TALES OF SOUTH JERSEY

TALES OF SOUTH JERSEY

PROFILES AND PERSONALITIES

Jim Waltzer & Tom Wilk

RUTGERS UNIVERSITY PRESS
NEW BRUNSWICK, NEW JERSEY

LIBRARY OF CONGRESS CATALOGING-IN-PUBLICATION DATA

Waltzer, Jim, 1950–
    Tales of south Jersey : profiles and personalities / by Jim Waltzer and Tom Wilk.
        p. cm.
    ISBN 0-8135-3006-7 (cloth : alk. paper) — ISBN 0-8135-3007-5 (pbk. : alk. paper)
        1. New Jersey—History, Local—Anecdotes.   2. New Jersey—Social life and customs—Anecdotes.   3. New Jersey—Biography—Anecdotes.   I. Wilk, Tom.   II. Title.
F134.6 .W35 2001
974.9—dc21   2001019289

British Cataloging-in-Publication data for this book is available from the British Library.

INTERIOR DESIGN: Judith Martin Waterman

Manufactured in the United States of America

To my mother,
my wife, Elizabeth,
and my daughters, Maria and Julia — T.W.

✦

To Helen and Sam Silberman — J.W.

Contents

Illustrations

Acknowledgments

Many of the chapters in this book were originally published as articles in *Atlantic City* magazine.

Any book is a collaborative effort. *Tales of South Jersey* could not have been written without the help of the following people, places, and organizations: Harold Abrams; Bill Ade; Anglers Club archives and members Tony Blundi, Bill Pellegrini, Ed Swirsky, and Gene Zaccaria; Skeetz Apel; Archdiocese of Philadelphia; Atlantic City Free Public Library and staffers Julie Senack and Diane Bitler; Atlantic City Historical Museum; *Atlantic City* magazine and publisher Joan Praiss and editors Ken Weatherford, Deborah Ein, Laura Albert, Paula Rackow, and Mike Epifanio; Atlantic County Historical Society; Melodye Bates-Holden; Blue Acorn Press; Dick Boccelli; Sherry Bowne; Boyer Museum; Jacob Brackman; Robert Bright; Robert Bright Jr.; *The Courier-Post*; *The County Press*; Grace D'Amato; The Down Jersey Folklife Center; Jim Fraser; Malcolm Fraser; Free Library of Philadelphia; Arnette Webster French; Willie Gainer; Gloucester County Historical Society; James Goslin; Tim Haggerty; Patti Harris; Sarah Hart; Jack Haynie; Mary Donaldson Haynie; Skip Hidlay; Ed Hitzel; Edith Hoelle; Tom Hulme; Ed Hurst; the International Clamshell Pitching Club of Cape May; Gilbert Katz; Helene Lehrman Katz; Bill Kelly; Herb Krassenstein; John Kurtz; Anthony Kutschera; Max Manning; David Maxwell; New Jersey State Museum in Trenton (1995–1996 exhibition "Signs of the Times"); New York Public Library (Library for Performing Arts, Schomburg Center for Research in Black Culture); Don Nyce; Ocean City Public Library; Louis Off; Philadelphia Toboggan Company; Dr. Jonathan Pitney House and Don Kelly; Princeton University; Bob Ruffolo; Frank Ruggieri; Sally Sachs; Paul Saxton; John Scanlon; Robert J. Scully; Seabrook Educational and Cultural Center; Skee-Ball Inc.; Mark Soifer;

The Southern New Jersey All Sports Museum and Hall of Fame; Sid Trusty; U.S. Patent and Trademark Office; Jim Usry; Penelope Watson; radio station WPEN; Bill Yorke.

Special thanks to Vicki Gold Levi and to Judith Martin Waterman of Martin-Waterman Associates and Alison Hack, Marlie Wasserman, and Marilyn Campbell of Rutgers University Press.

TALES OF SOUTH JERSEY

Introduction

G oing "down the shore" has long been a summer preoccupation of Philadelphians and humidity-oppressed residents of numerous other towns across the East Coast landscape. Nearly one hundred and fifty years ago, Atlantic City rose from the sands as the antidote to urban heat and soot, an elixir said to confer robust health and high spirits. In short order, it became the Queen of America's Resorts, courting vacationers with oceanfront palaces, all manner of fleshly and psychic diversions, and the salubrious salt air.

That the seashore dish turned out to be less nutritious than advertised, and the queenly reign somewhat shorter than Victoria's, does not negate the feverish attraction that this serendipitous slice of coastline once held (and, in varying degrees, still does) for pleasure seekers from hither and yon. "Down the shore" is a destination not easily discarded.

There is, of course, much more to southern New Jersey than Atlantic City. Other seashore communities are rich in history and an undeniable appeal for the homespun or the hell-raiser. Oceanside and bayside hamlets alike offer a box seat from which to observe the wonders of nature: marching crabs, migratory birds, littoral drifts. And the landlocked towns boast their own traditions and idiosyncracies quite apart from the seashore's summery lure.

So this excursion down the shore expands your horizons to include all of "Down Jersey" (the state's eight southernmost counties), which, for an eighteenth-century sailor, meant plenty of good fishing grounds, if a regrettable absence of lighthouses. Down this way, farms and ethnic neighborhoods and small-town flavor join the resorts and barrier islands. And whatever spot you pick—from the shores of the Delaware River to the beaches of the Atlantic Ocean—it will have a good tale to go with it.

For this book is not a travelogue, but a compendium of stories that illuminate, we hope, the region's character and eccentricity. Here you'll meet many of the personalities that shaped the profile of this sometimes brazen, sometimes quaint patch of the Eastern Seaboard. The focus will be Atlantic City and its outsize people, structures, and events. But the storytelling ranges across the wider region to provide an insider's look at history as it was being made—center-stage and beyond the footlights. You'll encounter gangsters and gamblers, hitters and hurricanes, famous piers and hotels, landmark theaters and eateries, splashy events and unheralded oddities—in sum, a cross-section of regional character and characters.

And each tale is in the telling.

ENTERTAINMENT

The Broadway Theatre

Whisper of how I'm yearning
to mingle with the old time throng.
Give my regards to old Broadway
and say that I'll be there, 'ere long!

—from *Little Johnny Jones*, George M. Cohan, 1904

On a warm spring evening, an eager crowd lined up outside the Broadway Theatre in downtown Pitman. It was May 18, 1926, and the excitement was building among the men, women, and children, many dressed in their Sunday best. Actor Thomas Meighan was starring in *The New Klondike*, a silent movie. Also on the bill were four vaudeville acts and music by the Broadway Orchestra. Tickets were thirty-five cents for the balcony and fifty cents for the main floor.

This was more than an evening's diversion. It marked the debut of the Broadway as an entertainment showplace and centerpiece of Pitman's business district. *The New Klondike* left after two days, but the Broadway stayed, entertaining customers for more than three-quarters of a century. Today, it is one of New Jersey's last single-movie theaters.

Located between a drugstore and a small recording studio on the east side of Broadway opposite Second Avenue, the Broadway, which seats just over a thousand people, remains a fixed point in a changing world. Like a hero in an old-time movie serial, the theater has survived real-life cliffhangers, including fires and bankruptcy. From television

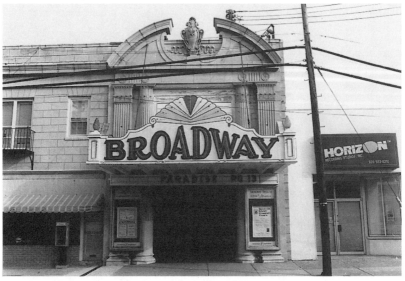

The Broadway Theatre has been a centerpiece of Pitman's business district since it opened in May 1926. It is one of the last remaining single-movie theaters in the state.
PHOTOGRAPH COURTESY OF THE *COURIER-POST*

to cable TV to the advent of videocassette recorders, DVD players, and the Internet, the Broadway has endured more challenges to its survival than Harrison Ford as Indiana Jones in *Raiders of the Lost Ark*.

The Broadway, built for an estimated $250,000, has been showing movies for so long that motion picture pioneer Thomas Edison was still alive when the theater admitted its first paying customer.

Although contemporary multiplexes, some with more than two dozen screens, dwarf it in size, none can match the Broadway for its rich show business history. Entertainers such as Bob Hope, Bing Crosby, Edgar Bergen, Sally Rand, Red Skelton, Jackie Gleason, and Abbott and Costello all performed on the theater's stage during the heyday of vaudeville. During the 1970s and 1980s, theater owner Clayton "Duffy" Platt revived the tradition of live entertainment, bringing in such country music stars as Crystal Gayle, Roy Clark, Charlie Pride, and Tammy Wynette and comedians such as Henny Youngman and Martin Mull. Three future members of the Rock and Roll Hall of Fame—Rick Nelson, Jerry Lee Lewis, and Johnny Cash—all performed at the Broadway before appreciative audiences in the 1980s.

The Broadway is a throwback to neighborhood movie houses and evokes the spirit of movie palaces of the 1930s and 1940s. A sense of history still pervades the Broadway. From its original chandeliers to its elevated guest boxes, from its spacious balcony to its Grand Kimball Theatre Organ, the Broadway would still be recognizable to a patron who had come on opening night. The Broadway's orange neon marquee still serves as a nighttime beacon in the Gloucester County borough of almost ten thousand residents.

Inside the Broadway, handrails covered in purple velvet and walls decorated in red-and-gold threaded silk complement the theater's Victorian architecture.

The key to the Broadway's longevity has been its seventy-two-foot stage. Live performances have been as much a part of the theater's history as popcorn and candy at the concession stand. After its opening, the theater quickly established itself as a stop on the East Coast vaudeville circuit between Philadelphia and Baltimore. The chance to see established stars and newcomers on the rise helped to keep customers in the seats during the Depression of the 1930s. Longtime movie projectionist Al Beckett kept track of the Broadway's performers by scrawling the names of each night's performers on the walls of the projection room.

Even though silent films dominated its early years, original Broadway owner, Ralph Wilkins, adapted to the advent of motion pictures with sound. The first talkie presented at the Broadway was *Alias Jimmy Valentine* starring Lionel Barrymore in 1929.

Vaudeville performances at the Broadway died off during World War II because of travel restrictions and changing tastes in entertainment. After the war, the rise of television posed a new challenge to movie theaters. The Broadway faced the challenge by maintaining low ticket prices and indulging in some gimmicks, such as the presentation of 3-D films like *House of Wax* starring Vincent Price. Moviegoers wore special glasses to make the movie appear three-dimensional.

The Broadway continued to host the occasional live event during the 1950s. Actor Preston Foster, a native of Ocean City and former Pitman resident, came to the theater in 1955 to help the borough celebrate its fiftieth anniversary. Foster, a strapping leading man, appeared in a hundred films, including *The Informer* and *Guadalcanal Diary*, and starred

With its elevated box seats and antique pipe organ
the Broadway Theatre is a throwback to movie theaters of an earlier era.
PHOTOGRAPH COURTESY OF THE *COURIER-POST*

in two television series, *Waterfront* and *The Gunslinger*, during an acting career that spanned forty years.

In August 1968, the Broadway suffered smoke and water damage in a blaze that killed one firefighter and also damaged a hardware store, jewelry shop, and pharmacy. More than two hundred firefighters fought this blaze. In September 1974, a fire broke out in an air-conditioning unit, causing only minor damage to the theater.

The Broadway changed hands in 1969 when the Wilkins family, which had operated the theater since 1926, sold it to Platt. As a child, Platt had seen Edgar Bergen and his dummy sidekick Charlie McCarthy perform at the theater. In 1977, with the memory of that show in mind, Platt revived the tradition of live performances with a series of country music concerts.

Singer Donna Fargo ("The Happiest Girl in the U.S.A.") was the inaugural performer. Other major country acts followed including Marty Robbins, the Oak Ridge Boys, and Tom T. Hall. Platt found he was filling a need for a concert venue in South Jersey. He built a mailing list of ten thousand patrons from New York to Virginia, eager to see concerts in an intimate space. Encouraged by the success of the country music shows, Platt began to books acts outside the genre, including Theodore Bikel, Leon Russell, Judy Collins, the Lettermen, and Dr. Hook and the Medicine Show.

Platt indulged in a bit of nostalgia in July 1979, when he brought back an evening of vaudeville entertainment with *Here It Is—Burlesque* starring Ann Corio, Morey Amsterdam, and Pinky Lee. Amsterdam, best known for his role as Buddy Sorrell on *The Dick Van Dyke Show*, drew laughs during the show when he remarked, "When I appeared on this stage forty-six years ago, the people liked my act so much, they just couldn't wait to bring me back!"

During the 1980s, Platt began to lose money on his concert presentations and filed for bankruptcy in 1985 with more than $80,000 owed in unpaid debts and back taxes. He nonetheless kept the Broadway open as a movie theater while working out a way to satisfy his creditors.

The Broadway also served the community as the site of the annual Miss Pitman pageant and, during the 1990s, as a house of worship. Platt rented the theater to the Gloucester County Community Church for its services before the congregation moved to its permanent home in neighboring Washington Township. Thus, for one weekend in 1993, it was possible to see Clint Eastwood star in *Unforgiven* on Saturday and be the forgiven on Sunday.

In 1999 Platt sold the Broadway to Dan Munyon and Charles Kern. The future of the Broadway appears to be bright; the theater has been renovated and the sound system has been upgraded. Community support remained strong, and customers could be seen lining up on weekends to attend a movie.

The new owners brought live entertainment back to the Broadway in 2000, catering to an older crowd by featuring such stars as Mickey Rooney and Al Alberts.

Since the early 1990s, volunteer workers for the Southern New Jersey Theatre Organ Society have been restoring the Broadway's venerable organ. The work has been painstaking and includes replacing the parts and doing a general overhaul of the instrument's more than six hundred pipes.

When the work is complete, the Broadway will have come full circle. Munyon and the society hope to present silent films with the restored organ providing the musical accompaniment just as it did on opening night in 1926. With support like this, the Broadway will not be fading to black any time soon.

Diving Duos

It is a gangway to the heavens. The wooden planks climb upward, upward, to a perch where the beautiful young woman awaits. Below, streamers flutter in the ocean breeze, and the crowd buzzes in the bleachers. For the moment, wide-eyed kids forget about their cotton candy.

Then, a flash of movement at the base of the tower; the staccato of horse hoofs on wood; the animal's flanks gleaming in the sun. He clip-clops to the top, and as he enters the chute, the young woman—a goddess in a one-piece bathing suit—takes him in stride, gripping the

*Poetry and peril: Arnette Webster plunges with
her mount John the Baptist from the diving tower into the pool on Steel Pier.*
PHOTOGRAPH COURTESY COLLECTION OF VICKI GOLD LEVI

reins as his forelegs slide onto the wooden apron angled downward
like an open trapdoor.

They milk the moment, pausing at the precipice, unfazed by the
gasps below. Then they are falling through space, falling in slow motion it seems, poetry and peril framed against the sky's sweeping canvas. They plunge forty feet into a broad pool twelve feet deep,
unleashing a giant splash a split-second before the crowd's roar of relief. Horse and rider bob to the surface, intact and glistening.

As the audience pours out its adulation, no one suspects that the
beautiful young rider is blind.

High-diving horses and their riders enthralled the paying customers at
Atlantic City's Steel Pier from 1929 to 1978, and, of the riders, Sonora
Webster Carver lasted the longest: fourteen years, eleven without the

benefit of eyesight. Timing, courage, and an affinity for the four-legged half of the act guaranteed her long run. Arnette Webster French followed her sister to the high-diving platform in an era when the Steel Pier presented bears on bicycles and "Rex" the Wonder Dog piloting his aquaplane. But the true stars of the show were the diving quarter horses: white-coated John the Baptist, the pinto Red Lips, the sorrel Klatawah. And their intrepid riders received equal billing.

The stunt was the brainchild of Dr. William Frank Carver, doctor of marksmanship and Wild West shows, a friend and business associate of "Buffalo Bill" Cody. According to legend, Carver conceived the idea one starry night when his horse tumbled through a soft spot in a country bridge, then reveled in the cool currents of the river below. A study in thigh-high boots and shoulder-length red hair, Doc Carver died two years before his diving steeds came to Steel Pier. But by that time, his daughter Lorena—the original diving-horse rider—and Sonora Webster had popularized the attraction at state and county fairs across the country.

Sonora was the eldest of six children born to Lila and Ula Webster in Waycross, Georgia. When Dr. W. F. Carver brought his show to nearby Savannah for a date in 1923, he interviewed prospective new riders at the Savannah Hotel. "My mother saw the ad in the paper—something about horses and travel," said Pleasantville resident Arnette French in 1997. "Sonora loved horses, but she didn't want to go [at first]."

She went . . . to Durham, North Carolina, for training, and on to live shows in Florida and California. Five years later, at age fifteen, Arnette joined the expanding show in Providence, Rhode Island, then headed west with Lorena Carver for performances in Oklahoma and Texas. Meanwhile, Sonora stayed on the New England circuit under the auspices of new husband Al Carver, son of the late W. F.

The next year, Steel Pier owner Frank Gravatt booked the eye-catching act and built a tower and tank to accommodate it. This was the ultimate venue for the High Diving Horses, one surrounded by ocean and kissed by the sky, a sun-spangled drama at pier's end. Then, in 1931, the dramatic turned tragic, but only for the moment.

In *Wild Hearts Can't Be Broken*, the touching 1991 Disney movie about Sonora's life, the crash of cymbals spooked her horse into an awkward dive. But in Arnette's telling, her sister "was fascinated by the horse's shadow going down. She hit the water with her eyes open. . . . She said it stung, but didn't hurt that bad. The doctor said it would clear up in a few days, and she kept on working. But when she kept losing vision, she went to a different doctor."

An operation failed to repair Sonora's detached retinas. Yet she was back on the high tower the very next season, performing on guts and memory . . . and with a sure hand. When she toured Cuba in the mid-thirties, her condition known by then, fans dubbed her "Blind Venus"—a goddess, indeed.

Meanwhile, Arnette left the High Diving Horses for the Steel Pier's rousing water show, married one of that show's key operatives (Jake French), and appeared with the wondrous canine Rex on the pages of *Life* and *Look* magazines. Such images filled several large scrapbooks tucked away in her Pleasantville home, where the memories were as vivid as a high diver knifing through a summer afternoon. Like all of the riders, she had a special affection for the horses.

"John [the Baptist] did what I call a 'corkscrew' dive," she said. "He pulled it on every new rider—he did it on purpose. . . . He'd lie in the water with just the tip of his nose [showing]; you'd swear he was drowning. Then he'd fly out of the pool."

Steel Pier went dark during World War II, effectively ending the performing careers of Sonora and Arnette. The Hamid family, who had featured riderless diving elks and mules on the Million Dollar Pier, bought Steel Pier in 1945 and fetched Lorena Carver out of retirement to manage the High Diving Horses show. A new generation of divers graced the tower, including the late Marion Hackney, who dove for thirteen years, second only to Sonora. There exists a wonderful photograph of Marion aboard Dimah (Hamid spelled backward), horse and rider emerging from the swirling water, each with beaming smiles.

"Dimah was my favorite horse," said Sarah Hart, who, as Sarah Detwiler, was a diver in the show during the 1956–1957 seasons and sporadically in the early sixties. "He would hesitate, and his head would bob up and down." Dimah's theatrics made him a favorite of the crowd, too.

Sarah's story begins in her native Apopka, Florida (near Orlando), where she was never far from the water—"I could swim before I could walk," she remembered. The daughter of a U.S. cavalryman, she inherited her father's fondness for horses and rigorous outdoor activity. When she came to southern New Jersey to visit her grandparents in 1955, she saw the High Diving Horses in action for the first time.

"I thought, what a great summer job," said Sarah, "and I sent a note backstage to Lorena Carver, expressing interest."

The next year, Sarah received an invitation to audition, made the forty-foot dive on a cold spring day, and was "hired on the spot." In 1957, she doubled as a horse diver and a member of the Diving Collegians, an antic group that featured the comedic talents of Marion Hackney's father, Joe. Water shows of that era included the Binswanger Bathing Beauties, which numbered among its bodies beautiful a husky lad named Gene Hart, future voice of the Philadelphia Flyers ice hockey club and future husband of Sarah Detwiler.

Meanwhile, Gene's father, Charley, was busy producing and directing the water shows, importing circus performers from Europe, and devising an elevator to transport riders and/or horses to the top of the tower. Sarah recalled that both her younger sister and Gene's mother had stints aboard the plunging ponies as well.

Performing at the Steel Pier was very much a family affair. And the horses, as part of that family, received plenty of carrots and tender loving care. "[The act was] totally sanctioned by the SPCA," said Sarah. "I was comfortable with the animals—I never prodded them; when they'd roll over underwater, I'd go right with them."

They were a diverse lot, those diving horses. In addition to Dimah, Sarah remembered Gamal ("a fast horse"), Lorgah ("a farm animal with white spots"), and Deloro ("a palomino—he wouldn't take a rider, but dove by himself") with an affection usually reserved for close kin or bosom buddies. "It was a fun thing, and it brought a lot to my life," she said.

It is a sentiment shared by this unique gallery of athletes, whose epitome, Sonora Webster Carver, retained an embattled zest into her nineties. Wild hearts can't be broken.

The Apollo Theatre

Her movements are ethereal, but her real appeal is fleshly. Feet and midriff bare, pearls teasing the hollow just below her throat, she arches her braceleted serpentine arms, and behind the frou-frou's gauzy billow, her legs are sheer allure. Her face remains inscrutable, but her body speaks volumes.

This was Miss Ruth St. Denis onstage at the Apollo Theatre in the unabashed 1920s. Her "Dances of the East" offered Oriental exotica and universal erotica, capturing both critics and crowds. The Apollo too was notable for such dual success.

As a repository of legitimate theater and other popular art forms, the Apollo was a touchstone for vintage Atlantic City. In its heyday—the second and third decades of the last century—the theater was the premier showplace in the top "tryout town" in America. Any Broadway-bound production worth its greasepaint stopped at the seashore for a tuneup.

Although the Apollo welcomed the likes of vaudevillians and exotic dancers, its preferred guests were the leading lights of the American theater: the dramatic (Helen Hayes, the Barrymores), the comedic (W. C. Fields, Eddie Cantor, the Marx Brothers), the musical (Al Jolson, Ethel Waters), the light-footed (Fred Astaire, Bill "Bojangles" Robinson).

While the god Apollo's mythological domain included music and poetry, the aptly named theater might also have been called the Phoenix, since three times a new building rose from an ash heap at New York Avenue and the boardwalk. Backed by saltwater taffy purveyor Joseph F. Fralinger and flamboyant impresario John L. Young, originally an ambitious concert hall called the Academy of Music was erected on the site in 1892. When, for the first time, it burned down within days of its premiere show, it was rebuilt in six weeks and opened with a "precision" horse show. After six years of novelty acts, it again succumbed to fire, and this time Fralinger was left to rebuild alone, since the seemingly prescient Young and a third partner had sold their interests to him a week earlier. But the Taffy King's stick-to-it attitude prevailed, and the third incarnation of the Academy opened in July 1898, hosting the newfangled "moving pictures" and stage plays seeking or concluding a New York run.

Actor Clifton Webb, singer Libby Holman, and
comedian Fred Allen (first row, center) led the cast of this 1929 show at the Apollo.
PHOTOGRAPH COURTESY VICKI GOLD LEVI

Not for long. Fanned by ocean gusts, a conflagration in April 1902 consumed the Academy and several blocks of boardwalk property. Ironically, Young's Ocean Pier Theatre became the town's main try-out spot as Fralinger rebuilt once again—this time with brick, iron, and asbestos. To curry favor with the Gods of Luck, a name change was in order. So Apollo, the fair-haired boy from Mount Olympus, now was riding on a golden chariot above the proscenium of the new, elegant, ivory-and-green theater.

The Apollo's boardwalk frontage was more pedestrian. Flanked by a jeweler and an importer, it looked like a four-story row house—if you ignored the stately cantilevered marquee and an electric sign teth-ered to the triangular roofline. Second- and third-floor bay windows overlooked the promenade. Once through the doors, however, patrons were treated to something of a surprise: this was no simple parlor lead-ing to a living room, but an expansive theater whose draped stage shoul-dered upper boxes and faced a sea of seats.

Fralinger leased the Apollo to exhibitor Samuel F. Nixon, and for twenty years, the marquee proclaimed Nixon's Apollo Theatre. With a seating capacity of nearly two thousand, it immediately became At-lantic City's leading theater when it opened in April 1908 and, along with the nearby Globe, fueled the town's theater boom following World War I. On opening nights, the New York/Philadelphia theatrical crowd (including critics) descended in white tie and tails, jewels and furs. Shows typically previewed for a week. Literary giant F. Scott Fitzgerald tried his hand with drama; his play *The Vegetable* opened at the Apollo on November 19, 1923, for a one-week run. Show producers had names like Erlanger, Shubert, and Belasco. The Apollo auditorium rang with the glorious melodies of Jerome Kern, the peppy tunes of George M. Cohan, and the symphonic operettas of Victor Herbert and Sigmund Romberg. (Romberg's famous *The Student Prince* was titled *In Old Heidelberg* when it debuted at the Apollo with a cast of 150.) Comedian Marie Dressler convulsed audiences in *Tillie's Nightmare*. Beautiful, star-crossed Jeanne Eagels played Sadie Thompson. George White's *Scandals* and the *Ziegfeld Follies* came to town.

It was Broadway by the beach.

But by the early 1930s, the bright lights were dimming. The Apollo was dark for most of the 1932–1933 season as the Depression took hold. Soon enough, though, like any great star, the Apollo reinvented itself.

With the proliferation of less expensive boardwalk entertainment and the growing popularity of the "talkies," live theater at the Apollo faced increasing competition for a dwindling dollar. Producers found cheaper ways to test their wares (e.g., summer stock), and Philadelphia, Boston, Hartford, and New Haven developed into more financially hospitable tryout towns. The Apollo hibernated for awhile, then reemerged in 1934. More spacious and with a new mezzanine, the theater cooled summer patrons with "purified air" pumped through a network of pipes. Sculpture commanded the wings and murals graced the walls. The most ambitious mural featured Apollo among a newfound cast of muses: Virgil, Plato, Socrates, Homer, Aristotle, Dante, and Shakespeare. The God of Music thrummed his lyre, while the muses . . . mused.

The theater's prime display was not quite so contemplative. The deepened, widened stage now boasted the state's largest movie screen enlivened by "wide range" sound—the Apollo had gone Hollywood. The inaugural photoplay at the converted theater was *Nana*, a vehicle for glamorous Russian actress Anna Sten. Red-blooded American stars like Cagney, Gable, and Bette Davis would follow, perhaps the most compelling of them all spotlighted, generically, in the 1945 release *Story of G. I. Joe*.

Future films would prove less heroic. Signs of the theater's fate were apparent early on, for even as the Apollo's nobly evocative interior suggested high ideals, its front door sought a more common denominator. The marquee turned garish, as assorted billboards and screaming posters summoned the boardwalk foot traffic. Finally, the invitation became an outright leer. A flattened, downsized marquee announced "xxx" movies and the "Ms. Nude International Pageant." Smaller signs promised pizza and comics to go with "burlesk" [sic]. It was the mid-1970s, and T-shirts had replaced the furs and tuxes of yesteryear's opening nights.

The performance heirs of Ruth St. Denis had stripped the Apollo of artful pretense. Like a once beautiful movie star grotesquely painted in her dotage, the theater remained a burlesque house until 1978, when it shut its doors and awaited the wrecking ball. Deliverance didn't come until 1985.

High-rise condominiums now tower over the site. Burgundy storefront awnings are sedate descendants of the Apollo's vigorous marquee. The footlights have gone out. Stars, though, are loath to leave the stage. Sometimes, when the sky closes in and the ocean is quiet, a lost lyric or line of dialogue—like a seashell's trapped mystery—finds its way to your ear.

Club Harlem

The bandstand is blasting. Horns pour, a big bass thumps the beat, and the drummer cooks, tattooing the cymbals as punctuation. In front of the musicians, sinuous dancers command a tub-shaped stage below which tables sit atop the patterned carpet. The dancers tease the music, as silhouettes painted on wall mirrors undulate in the shifting light. Dazzled patrons at red-and-black booths lean into the intoxication of the night . . . Saturday night, or to be precise, Sunday morning—the wee small hours.

And there is still another show to come.

The address was 32 North Kentucky Avenue, and it was a place where the night never died. If the whole block—including jazz spots Grace's Little Belmont and the Wonder Garden bar—was a magnet

The outside was pedestrian, but inside there was magic: Club Harlem in April 1972.
PHOTOGRAPH COURTESY OF THE *COURIER-POST*

for celebrities and night-life connoisseurs, Club Harlem was its center. The music roared like nowhere else. Sunday morning (five A.M.) "breakfast" shows kept the house packed, though breakfast was little more than pretzels and a chaser. Headliners from the Steel Pier and the 500 Club arrived after their gigs and, sometimes, took the stage to do their act for free. This was home to the Sepia Revue, Smart Affairs, the Beige Beauts of ornate headdresses and long leg-lines, dapper men, elegant women, and the best musicians on the planet.

Through the years, the roster at Club Harlem read like a Who's Who of black entertainers. There were classics (Billie Holiday, Joe Williams), crooners (Lou Rawls, Brook Benton), comics (Dick Gregory, George Kirby), and "Crazy" Chris Columbo on drums. There were belters (Dinah Washington, Aretha Franklin), beauties (Leslie

Uggams, Damita Jo), barn burners (Cab Calloway, Al Hibbler), and Billy Daniels weaving his "Ole Black Magic." Sammy Davis Jr. danced onstage when his age was still in single digits. Salty comedian "Moms" Mabley spouted shockers and wore her signature squashed hat.

And there were lesser names who were just as memorable. "Hot Lips" Page blew a mean trumpet, alluring Chinkie Grimes danced with exotic flair, and the redoubtable Clayton "Peg Leg" Bates danced on . . . you guessed it.

Crowds were integrated, but aside from a Paul Whiteman or a Lenny Bruce, Club Harlem was a showcase for black talent. Founder Leroy "Pop" Williams once said that he decided on the name "Harlem" because "a lot of black people live there." Excitement, however, was color-blind on Kentucky Avenue.

Williams transformed a dance hall called Fitzgerald's Auditorium into Club Harlem in 1935, and the pedestrian exterior didn't even hint at the magic inside. Two lounges soon offered liquor and musical licks to stoke the crowd before the main show—indefatigable drummer Columbo often teamed with guitarist "Wonderful" Floyd Smith and jazz organist "Wild Bill" Davis before hitting the big room, which sat nine hundred without testing the fire ordinance. Columbo piloted the house band for thirty-four straight summers at Club Harlem. Of Davis, he once said, "He brought the Hammond organ from the funeral homes and gave it to jazz."

In the early days, Club Harlem was alive with more than just music. The manager was reputed to be a former bootlegger, and by day, the establishment took bets on the ponies; blackjack and craps games beckoned from a backroom in an adjacent building.

But the enduring commerce here was show biz: unmatched music, sleek dancers, and comics peeling off lines like Slappy White's "my mother-in-law likes everything about me except my eyes—she can't stand the sight of me." Debonair promoter Larry Steele packaged his annual Smart Affairs tour for Miami Beach and Las Vegas as well as Club Harlem, and from the cabaret duskiness of singer Nancy Wilson to the vaudevillian zip of comic White, it all worked.

In 1951, Pop Williams and his brother, Clifton, recruited additional partners, including Ben Alten, who left the rival Paradise Club on Illinois Avenue. Years later, the *Atlantic City Press* quoted Alten as saying, "Pop wanted a white man as a partner, because he wanted to expand the place, and in those days, the banks weren't lending money to black men." Pop found his green, the walls turned to red-and-gold velvet, and the club continued to thrive. But even though the music was timeless, the club became a casualty.

The lot on which Club Harlem stood now seems unnatural space, a wound between the exposed brick walls of flanking buildings. In December 1992, a northeaster shook the structure and mangled the colorful sign—shaped like a musical note—above the marquee, its neon dormant for six years. A couple of weeks later, the historic building was razed.

The advent of casino-hotels had drawn the paying customers to the boardwalk, consigning the streetfront clubs to history. But years before the casino-hotels, in 1972, Club Harlem began its slide into oblivion. In the early morning hours of Easter Monday, a shootout inside the club triggered a melee and five deaths. Warring gangs from Philadelphia were the culprits, drugs their focus. Times were changing.

Before the bulldozer arrived, a few loyalists rescued some of the inimitable texture of Club Harlem: chairs, booths, padded interior doors, vintage photographs that adorned the walls, props used onstage. These materials await the day when they'll return to center stage, perhaps as part of a museum celebrating African-American history.

The annual Kentucky Avenue Renaissance Festival, held on and around the lot that was once Club Harlem, is a reminder of what was, and a suggestion of what can be. Nostalgia produces energy as surely as wistfulness. The daylong summer fair features food, artwork, visions of the future, and, of course, pulsating music. The very breath of Club Harlem.

This nightspot that housed the greatest entertainment in the world can't resist an encore.

Peg Leg Bates

The army chaplain was on the line, calling from the hospital. "Can you send him over for twenty minutes or so? The men would really love it."

Soldiers clogged the wards, the lucky ones in traction, the less fortunate, missing limbs. War still raged across the ocean, but just beyond the massive walls of Haddon Hall's Thomas England General Hospital, summertime bathers secured their beachheads with towels and blankets.

The dancer arrived at the hospital within half an hour. He had brought an accompanist who could extract magic from a keyboard—a man by the name of Bill "Count" Basie. The vets cheered, dead weight lifting from broken bodies. Then the show began, the keyboard dripping champagne notes, the dancer tapping on the hard hospital floor, his spontaneous routine rich in rhythm and joy and a courage that had become instinctive.

He danced in every ward, a five-hour performance of both tribute and self-affirmation. For as the men whistled and clapped and imagined the days when they could stomp their feet, the dancer's energy raced through them like an electrical current. He was a force field, indefatigable, unconquerable. And they wondered what he might have been—greater or lesser?—dancing on *two* legs.

When Clayton "Peg Leg" Bates played Atlantic City's swanky Paradise Club in the summer of 1943, he was already an international star. He had conquered Harlem (the Cotton Club), Broadway (the Paramount), Paris (the Moulin Rouge), and, in a command performance, the king and queen of England. But his most enthusiastic audience may have been the soldiers that afternoon nearly six decades ago at England General.

He danced, he jabbered, he danced some more. Nonstop. He made them laugh.

That was Peg Leg's supreme gift: to make people feel good. It was a gift earned by exuberance and an uncompromising will. "Don't judge me as a one-legged dancer," Bates once said. "Judge me as a dancer."

The dancing master: Peg Leg Bates
could do more on one leg than most could manage on two.
PHOTOGRAPH COURTESY MELODYE BATES-HOLDEN

By any number of measures, though, he was unique. His story eludes the most creative scriptwriter. Born in Fountain Inn, South Carolina, in 1907, Clayton Bates was a dancing prodigy by the age of five. Barefoot, he'd wander into the town barbershop and "buck" dance, clapping his hands to set the rhythm. Customers tossed pennies and nickels, but Clayton's Baptist sharecropper mother was offended by the spectacle and forbade her son to dance in public.

Soon a new imperative took center stage. With World War I claiming many of its laborers, the local cotton mill was shorthanded. Twelve-year-old Clayton Bates joined the workforce and pitchforked piles of cottonseed into threshing machinery for conversion to linseed oil—a raw material needed for the war effort. Working the graveyard shift one night, young Clayton stepped onto an open thresher. A co-worker heard the scream.

Black patients rarely went to hospitals in the rural South of 1919, and the maimed Clayton Bates wound up on his mother's kitchen table, where doctors amputated his chewed-up left leg eight inches below the knee. Two fingers from his right hand had already been severed by the accident.

But the young man's spirit was never less than whole. His uncle fashioned him a rudimentary peg leg, and eighteen months later, teenage Clayton Bates was walking to school and jumping over ditches. He returned to the scene of early glories—the barbershop—and shined shoes, rhythmically swishing the rags as he buffed. The sound was infectious, and there was no cure for what ruled his heart. He would use his peg like a drumstick to drive and punctuate the beat. He would dance again.

Amateur shows, then traveling troupes beckoned the seventeen-year-old Bates, who, more than once, was stranded when carnivals and minstrel shows went belly up. Hitchhiking one day in 1926, he was picked up by the private bus of Eddie Lemon and the "Dashing Dinah Revue." Promoter Lemon promptly added Bates to the show ticketed for Philadelphia and New York, and soon Bates was appearing at the Lafayette Theater in Harlem, and with Lew Leslie's famed "Blackbirds" on Broadway. The scenery had changed dramatically for Peg Leg Bates.

The innovative dancer quickly became a crowd favorite, tapping with expert rhythm and using the peg to launch and ground acrobatic, midair turns. With a metal tap on his shoe and the butt of his peg, a combination of leather (for sound) and rubber (for cushioning), Bates was an unforgettable blend of rhythmic mastery and muscular daring, his disdain for risk creating tantalizing drama. He could glide, whirl, high-step, tap out a fusillade, and leap like a power forward grabbing a rebound. He ended many a routine with his astonishing "Jet Plane," catapulting himself above the stage, landing full force on the peg, and hopping backward, the band saluting each hop with a trumpet blast. "He stopped every show," said Honi Coles, an equally legendary tap dancer.

One time at the Paradise Club, Bates stopped the show earlier than intended, when the "Jet Plane" crash-landed, and his peg leg shot through a knothole in the wooden floorboards. It took half an hour to extricate the dauntless dancer.

"I've gone through floors all over the world," he would say afterward. Peg Leg escaped and finished his act that night, and the Paradise stage was soon girded with a sheath of metal.

When the Paradise concluded its 1943 season, Bates and producer Ziggy Johnson expanded the show into the "Atlantic City Follies" and hit the road. In other years, Peg Leg played Atlantic City's Club Harlem, where he wowed Kentucky Avenue audiences with flips and handstands in addition to his regular repertoire.

Meanwhile, distant ports and more exotic stages were calling. Bates toured Australia with Louis Armstrong, rejoined Count Basie for a series of performances at Radio City Music Hall, and, in 1950, became the first black performer to appear on television's *Ed Sullivan Show*, a program he would grace twenty-two times, the last at age sixty.

As meticulous as he was dynamic, Bates had a New York designer make his peg legs in an assortment of colors, and donned tuxedos and top hats to match. In an altogether different getup, he became the crusty sea captain Long John Silver and danced up a storm on deck.

Indeed, elegance and earthiness claimed equal parts of this driven man, whose innovation reached beyond the dance floor. In 1951, Peg Leg Bates played Grossinger's in New York's Catskill Mountains and realized that the only blacks in sight were on the stage. He was hardly a stranger to racial separation, but now he conceived an entrepreneurial vision as bold as his gymnastic choreography: an integrated resort. So he purchased a seven-acre turkey farm in the Catskills and converted it to a country club in 1952. His wife, Alice, handled the administrative duties; later, his daughter, Melodye, joined him onstage in the club's showroom, the two of them closing their act with a shim sham.

The Peg Leg Bates Country Club never did achieve integration, though it was a haven for black vacationers. Ironically, the civil rights movement made it a dinosaur by opening the doors of other resorts to blacks. But not before Bates had proved himself adept at business.

He was quite a presence at the club—entertaining at night, roaming the grounds in a golf cart by day, pausing for snapshots with visitors. A pair of hip replacements slowed his pace, but just barely. In later years—in the mountains, New York City, and his old hometown—Bates became a messenger of good will and hard truths, speaking to youth groups, and raising money for schools and charity. And performing, even into the nineties, even into *his* nineties. Until his death in December 1998 in South Carolina, about a mile from the site of the accident that had taken his leg, he continued his morning regimen of stretching exercises, keeping that extraordinary body limber.

For Peg Leg Bates, the whole idea was to keep going, damn the odds.

On a magical afternoon in the Atlantic City of World War II, hundreds of hospitalized soldiers received that message, loud and clear.

The Crooner and the Comic

Waiters outnumbered patrons. Onstage, a male singer mutilated the melody. It was no surprise that the honcho had a headache. Paul "Skinny" D'Amato sat at a corner table and ground his teeth. One chair over, his $150-a-week comic commiserated. The young comedian had just done fifteen minutes of pantomiming well-known singers as their recordings spun in the wings. For the moment, his manic energy and rubbery features were in repose. His bow tie flared and his herringbone sports jacket hung on thin shoulders. An unruly pompadour rose from his forehead, which he massaged with the tips of his fingers.

Outside the club, a uniformed attendant stood idle underneath a three-sided marquee flanked by iron grates and awninged windows. He clung to a brick column and watched boxy cars disappear down Missouri Avenue into the summer night.

Back in the showroom, Skinny D'Amato squinted through a plume of smoke, as the croaking continued from the stage of his 500 Cafe. He squashed his butt and turned away.

"Know where I can get a singer?"

The comic straightened and looked at his boss; his eyes danced. Yeah . . . sure . . . he knew a singer.

Destiny often draws from modest beginnings. Skinny D'Amato grew up within shouting distance of the site of the future 500 Club, lost his father at a tender age, and ran a smoke shop in the 2200 block of Arctic Avenue when he was just fifteen. (The establishment was better known for backroom gambling than stogies.) Soon, the young entrepreneur was expert at finding safe havens for floating craps games and eventually took the reins at the gambling hall–nightclub Luigi's at Arkansas and Pacific avenues.

Meanwhile, ex-Philadelphia trolley conductor Phil Barr had been running a similar enterprise—the 500 Cafe at 6 South Missouri—since its opening in 1918. When Barr died in 1942, Skinny jumped to the "Fives," upgraded the menu and entertainment, and developed a fondness for silk ties and hand-stitched suits. High times lay ahead.

Joseph Levitch was born in March 1926 in Newark, and came of age in an ethnic neighborhood in nearby Irvington. His father was an itinerant entertainer–song plugger, his mother a piano player who "demonstrated" popular songs for shoppers at the S.S. Kresge five-and-dime. When their son hit the show biz circuit in earnest, he became Jerry Lewis.

He was still shy of his twentieth birthday and working at a Manhattan bistro called the Glass Hat when he was introduced by a mutual friend to a romantic balladeer with penetrating eyes and a Cary Grant hairline. Dean Martin's confident air had sprung from a hardscrabble background. Born Dino Crocetti in June 1917 in Steubenville, Ohio, he was the son of an immigrant barber, and a veteran of steel mills and gambling rooms before he was out of his teens. A soul brother to Skinny D'Amato; a big brother to Jerry Lewis.

Martin had patterned his mellow, off-the-rack singing style after Bing Crosby and the Mills Brothers, fronted a band in Cleveland, and then made his way to New York, where he sang on radio and met Lewis in March 1946. The two men shared an affinity for big dreams. They swapped autobiographies and funny stories in a little hotel room until the sun came up. Martin and Lewis shared the bill but performed separately at the Havana-Madrid, a basement club on Times Square. They began to horse around together onstage after their regular acts ended. They seemed perfect foils for each other.

Atlantic City moved to a nightclub beat in the summer of forty-six. On a night in late July, the Paradise offered a "girl revue," Club Harlem sizzled with cool jazz, a rhumba band held sway at the Bath and Turf, Babette's trotted out "Fifth Avenue models," and The Clicquot touted a "physcopathic [*sic*] MC." At the 500 Cafe, the supper club boasted the "finest chops" in town, and the musical bar featured "continuous entertainment," with the last show starting at four A.M. The headliner was the "gorgeous, unpredictable" singer-comedian Jayne Manners. As an "added attraction," Jerry Lewis did "satirical impressions in pantomimicry." Ms. Manners had the billing, but it was Lewis who was truly unpredictable.

Afternoons, Lewis sat on a boardwalk bench and worked out his act, while at the Steel Pier matinee, Harry James loosed golden trumpet notes over the ocean. On the night of July 24, Lewis blew Dean Martin's horn.

"He's a terrific singer," he told Skinny D'Amato, who winced as his current male vocalist groaned on. Skinny was not familiar with Martin.

"Not only that," Lewis continued with the prescience of a seer, "we do a lot of funny stuff. . . . We've worked together."

And they had—in a New York hotel room in the wee small hours just a couple of months earlier.

Skinny picked up the phone. The next night, Dean Martin was working at the Fives, billed below Miss Manners but above Jerry Lewis. The newspapers—full of the overheated, dubious revelations of press agents—welcomed the "Diamond Records artist," the "most recent Hollywood singing discovery," who represented "romance in song."

Dean Martin (top) did the singing and had great comedic timing; Jerry Lewis was the over-the-top clown. Together, they were a force on the American entertainment scene for a decade.

PHOTOGRAPH COURTESY OF THE *COURIER-POST*

He was said to be ticketed for the West Coast to make a movie and at the Shore for a "limited time."

For his first show, the crooner sang five songs. The comic came on and did his act. Neither outing was a blockbuster.

"Where's the funny stuff?" D'Amato asked afterward. The straight skinny: Be funny or else.

They conferred in the dressing room. Martin returned to the mike and glided through eight bars. Lewis donned a busboy's jacket and followed him onstage. Plates flew. Plates crashed. The band's sheet music went up in flames. Jerry bumped the accompanist off his stool, then jumped offstage and spilled a few goblets, making his patented monkey faces.

All the while, Dean sang. And the customers shrieked—for three hours.

That may be how it happened. In other tellings, the replaced singer had taken ill, the deliverer of the ultimatum was not Skinny but his partner Irvin Wolf, and the Martin-Lewis transformation didn't occur until the next day. Dean Martin's agent insisted it was his phone call that started it all.

Whatever preceded those madcap moments onstage, the future was ordained. Bigger crowds, then full houses, then lines down the boardwalk. Martin and Lewis doing their fake-drowning routine on the beach, and inviting spectators to see more at their nightclub show. The immortal, irreverent Sophie Tucker catching one of those shows and proclaiming the pair zanier than Abbott and Costello. There would be a month of their exhausting antics at the Fives, followed by dates at Philadelphia's Latin Casino and Loew's Capitol Theater in New York. The next year brought a triumphant return to Atlantic City and a twelve-week run at New York's famed Copacabana. Then on to Hollywood and sixteen hit films, the proverbial "hottest ticket in town" at nightclubs across the nation, airplanes taking them everywhere, menchildren on a rocket ride.

For Skinny D'Amato's nightclub, too, the ante had been raised. The greatest names in show business awaited: Durante, Berle, Gleason, Sammy Davis Jr., Nat "King" Cole, Tony Martin, and, of course, Sinatra. In the 1950s a shirt-sleeve crowd would press toward the canopied entrance, above which Skinny and his family had their living quarters, and a vertical sign now said "500 Club."

Nothing is forever. Martin and Lewis would make a movie called *Hollywood or Bust* in 1956, and promptly bust up—ten years, almost to the day, after their genesis. Martin would surprise by holding his own on-screen with the likes of Marlon Brando and John Wayne, become a charter member of the Rat Pack, make more hit records, and conquer television with a weekly variety show. Lewis would become *The Bellboy* and *The Nutty Professor*, and other loonies, write and direct his own material, gain legendary stature in France, and touch hearts with the annual Muscular Dystrophy Telethon.

There would be endings come too soon. The 500 Club would burn to the ground on June 10, 1973 (the Trump Plaza garage now stands on the site), and death would claim Skinny D'Amato at age seventy-five in June 1984 and Dean Martin in December 1995.

But all of that was a lifetime away one July night in 1946, when magic visited a little club on Missouri Avenue and changed the entertainment landscape.

Bill Haley: Rockin' around South Jersey

John Anthony stood in back of the Twin Bar, his Gloucester City club, surveyed the stage, and raised his hands to his ears with mixed emotions. The Saddlemen, the musical group he had hired, could pack the place, no easy feat in a city with more than twenty bars. It was the middle of the Korean War and sailors from the Philadelphia Naval Base poured across the river into his tavern like draft beer into a glass. However, the group's lead guitarist and singer seemed intent on setting a world record for how loudly he could play his instrument.

The Saddlemen were a country-and-western band, but they would often veer off into a type of music that Anthony never heard before—a heavily amplified rhythm with screaming vocals that the guitarist called "cowboy jive," whatever that was. All he could make out of the lyrics was the line, "We're gonna rock this joint tonight." By this point, Anthony's patience had worn thin. Pushing and apologizing as he made his way through the crowd, Anthony got to the edge of the horseshoe-shaped stage, hopped onto it, and, to the amusement of the band, turned down the amplifier as the song concluded.

The young guitarist, named Bill Haley, cracked a small smile as he acknowledged Anthony's presence. After the Twin Bar owner left the stage, Haley's fingers imperceptibly turned up the volume control as the band swung into its next number.

In the revolution of popular music, lines were being drawn. South Jersey would serve as the musical version of Lexington and Concord.

From the Delaware River to the Atlantic Ocean, Bill Haley would use South Jersey as a springboard to musical success. Those years of constant touring between 1951 and 1955 would turn the Saddlemen (later renamed the Comets) into a top-flight group and make Haley the first international rock 'n' roll star. Whether it be at Andy's Log Cabin outside Camden, the Hofbrau Tavern in Wildwood, or Atlantic City's Steel Pier, Haley merged black music (rhythm and blues) and white music (country and western) to produce rock 'n' roll through such songs as "Rock the Joint," "Shake, Rattle, and Roll" and "Rock around the Clock."

"We use country-and-western instruments, play rhythm-and-blues tunes, and the result is pop music," Haley said in a 1955 interview. In an era highlighted by Patti Page's "How Much Is That Doggie in the Window" and Eddie Fisher's "Oh! My Pa-Pa," Haley's ascent would signal major changes on the musical horizon.

Haley was an unlikely rock 'n' roll hero. He lacked the overt sexuality of Elvis Presley (Haley was nearly a decade older) or the visual outrageousness of Little Richard. Blind in his left eye and nearsighted in his right, Haley was forced by a lack of depth perception to limit his movements onstage. Nevertheless, he possessed qualities that could not be seen with the naked eye—a strong will and a burning desire to succeed in the music business. A struggling country singer since the mid-1940s—he once was billed as "Yodeling Bill Haley"—the one-time Salem resident and Delaware Valley disk jockey was not afraid to experiment and carve out a musical career on his own terms.

The experimentation also meant new ways of bringing his music to the public. Haley performed live radio shows on WPWA-AM, a Chester, Pennsylvania–based radio station heard across the Delaware River in South Jersey. More importantly, he brought his music to people who could not see him in clubs—teenagers. Haley, his manager, Lord Jim Ferguson, and the other members of the band (bassist Marshall Lytle, steel guitarist Billy Williamson, and accordionist/pianist Johnny

Grande) felt teenagers would make an eager audience for their new sounds. Since teenagers were not old enough to come to the clubs, Haley brought the music to them, performing at high-school assemblies free of charge.

The philosophy of "have band, will travel" brought the group to auditoriums, gymnasiums, and cafeterias at more than a hundred and fifty schools. "Rock the Joint," Haley's theme song at the Twin Bar, was an immediate hit with the students. Its release as a single in April 1952 convinced Haley he was moving in the right direction: It became his biggest seller to date.

School assemblies proved to be an invaluable marketing technique. Haley and the band kept a close eye on their young audience to see what was working and, more importantly, what wasn't.

After one show in 1953, Haley and Lytle were talking to the students to see what they thought of the show. One student said: "It was crazy, man, crazy." The phrase stuck in their heads and Haley and Lytle wrote a song based on that phrase in one afternoon. Released in April 1953 on the local Essex label, "Crazy, Man, Crazy" became the group's first Top 20 single.

As Haley's success grew, so did the band. The additions of drummer Dick Richards and saxophonist Joey D'Ambrose brought the band up to six members. They became a common fixture at the Jersey Shore from 1953 to 1955, playing a variety of venues from the Shelter Haven Hotel in Stone Harbor to Hunt's Pier in Wildwood.

For Haley, the shore was an ideal place to indulge his twin passions of fishing and music. Days were devoted to fishing—he was the epitome of patience at the end of a fishing line—as Haley thought nothing of spending hours on the Atlantic Ocean in the *Comet*, a boat that was a gift from his fellow band members for his twenty-ninth birthday in July 1954.

Nights, though, were devoted to music. During the summer of 1954, the band held court from Memorial Day to Labor Day at the Hofbrau in Wildwood.

The band was entering its peak period, and Haley allowed the versatility of his group to shine through. Lytle and Richards each got a vocal solo while Williamson did a comedy routine.

The Comets developed a visual flair and a knack for showmanship. Lytle had discovered his twenty-five-pound, upright bass could be used

Bill Haley (top) and His Comets used South Jersey as a launching pad for their career in the 1950s. Haley was inducted into the Rock and Roll Hall of Fame in 1987.

PHOTOGRAPH COURTESY OF THE *COURIER-POST*

for more than just music. He would lie the instrument on its side and jump astride it while continuing to keep the beat. Later, he developed a routine with D'Ambrose in which he would push his bass across the stage while the sax player hitched a ride atop it and played his solo.

To break up the grind of playing seven days a week, the Comets kept their act fresh with such antics as playing an occasional show in their swimming trunks. This type of hijinks added a new dimension to the band when competition among the shore clubs—featuring acts from the Treniers to Tony Bennett—was strong. The Hofbrau was nearly always filled to its capacity of five hundred people.

On the recording front, Haley and the Comets signed with Decca Records, a major label that would ensure better distribution of their records. Although the first single released by Decca, "Rock around the Clock" was initially a flop, the next one, "Shake, Rattle, and Roll," released in July 1954, was a Top 10 hit.

The group's repertoire at the Hofbrau was built around "Rock the Joint," "Crazy, Man, Crazy," and "Shake, Rattle, and Roll." Ironically, the seeds of the group's eventual breakup took root as Haley began to taste national success. Financial squabbles would increase with the worldwide success of "Rock around the Clock" in 1955. (It would stay at number 1 on *Billboard Magazine*'s singles chart for eight weeks.) The newer members of the band—Lytle, Richards, and D'Ambrose—felt they deserved a raise but were denied one. The trio gave notice they were leaving the Comets on Labor Day 1955, following a concert at Hunt's Pier in Wildwood. The first edition of the Comets came to an end on the unofficial last day of summer.

Haley continued on with new bandmates, but he would soon be overshadowed by other rock 'n' roll stars who followed, including Elvis Presley, Chuck Berry, and Buddy Holly. But Haley, who was inducted into the Rock and Roll Hall of Fame in 1987, had established a musical sound and direction in defiance of the tastes and commercial standards of the times. In later years, his role in the development of rock would be played down, a fact that would bother him until his death in February 1981.

"The story has got pretty crowded as to who was the father of rock 'n' roll," he said in a 1970s interview. "I haven't done much in life except that, and I'd like to get credit for it."

The Voice of the Shore

The boy announcer lowered his head onto the desk and fell asleep. It had been another late night on the air, and nodding off in fifth-period Spanish class was becoming a pattern. Soon enough, the sixteen-year-old found himself in the Atlantic City High School principal's office, where he was given a choice: leave the radio station or leave school.

"I made my decision," recalled Ed Hurst, who began his broadcast career as a high-school junior at Atlantic City's then NBC-affiliate WFPG (World's Famous Playground) and was still behind the mike nearly six decades later.

He eventually dropped out of school to join the navy, though he did return to graduate. He also returned to the airwaves, as ambition and timing conspired to make his a household name around the regional (and sometimes national) dial.

Regardless of what the calendar says, whenever Ed Hurst's friendly voice rides the radio, it is summertime. Tots dredge by the shoreline, ice-cream vendors patrol the sands, and the Steel Pier is jumpin'.

The broadcaster grew up on Oriental Avenue in Atlantic City's colorful Inlet neighborhood, his father a local attorney who once contested a state senate seat with the imposing Hap Farley, his mother a Curtis Institute–trained pianist. Son Ed drew qualities from both, building a career that demonstrated a way with people and an ear for music.

The radio show that sent the young Hurst into repeated afternoon slumber in 1943 was called "Night Trick," a seven P.M. to one A.M. network-feed broadcast from the Steel Pier. Staff announcer Hurst introduced musical recordings, a task he also performed at occasional remotes from the Knickerbocker Hotel and the nightclub Paddock International, the latter featuring the Ten Flying Fingers of (pianist) Bob Bell. Before enlisting in the navy the next year, Hurst would broadcast the big-band sounds of Teddy Powell, saxophonist Charlie Barnett, and trumpeter Harry James live from the Steel Pier's Marine Ballroom. "It

*For millions of listeners, it
seemed as though Ed Hurst
invented the summer sounds on
the Steel Pier.*
PHOTOGRAPH COURTESY OF
THE *COURIER-POST*

was right before he [James] married Betty Grable," said Hurst. "I looked
so young, they didn't want to let me backstage to do the show."

In one instance that required sight as well as sound, Hurst moved
his equipment to the window and described a fire that swept across
Virginia and Maryland avenues.

After completing his stint with Uncle Sam, Hurst returned to WFPG
and the "133 Club," a mix of soaps, music, and "three minutes of news
at 1:30 P.M." But the young announcer sought to expand his radio horizons. He moved in with his sister in Miami and landed a job at station
WIOD (Wonderful Island of Dreams), then promptly sent audition tapes
to three Philadelphia stations. The twenty-year-old Hurst was hired by
WPEN—then owned by the *Evening Bulletin*—in 1946 and put on the air
at five A.M. "doing symphonic music and news." The early hours
couldn't suppress the young man's flair.

"I came up as a personality," said Hurst, who, in his mid-seventies,
still brought a sense of informality and occasional devilment to his pro-
gramming. "The afternoon guy, Joe Grady, was strait-laced and had a
squeaky-voiced partner. . . . They paired us [Grady and Hurst] for a six-
week trial, and we took off together."

Their show, the "950 Club" (WPEN is at 950 on the AM dial), became Philadelphia's top-rated radio program for an entire decade. During that stretch, the duo also ventured into television, hosting two dance shows and *The Plymouth Showroom*, a variety program spotlighting popular recording artists. Hurst was forming lasting ties with the likes of Tony Bennett, Nat "King" Cole, Frankie Lane, and Patti Paige. One prime opportunity, however, escaped the team of Grady and Hurst. In the early fifties, media mogul Walter Annenberg tried to recruit the pair for a "dance party" show to be simulcast on his Philadelphia radio and TV stations, but according to Hurst, WPEN held fast to their contracts, and the station's new owner—Sun Ray Drugs, a major chain at the time—threatened to move its advertising from Annenberg's *Inquirer* to the *Bulletin*. The dance show, a precursor to *American Bandstand*, nonetheless was launched, but without Grady and Hurst. In short order, an announcer named Dick Clark came aboard, and the show soared into rock 'n' roll legend.

But Ed Hurst had plans for his own signature show, one with a distinctively seashore flavor.

It is 1965, and the world is not without turmoil. There's a perplexing war overseas, civil unrest grips the South, and the New York Yankees' baseball dynasty is finally crumbling. But on the beach, the sands are serene and the infectious warbling of Herman's Hermits slips out of transistor radios. On television, Ed Hurst presides over *Summertime at the Pier*, and teens move in tandem with the dancing surf.

The pier, of course, is the Steel Pier; the announcer is back in the Marine Ballroom. Hurst's June–to–Labor Day, Saturday afternoon songfest is in its eighth season. It will air another dozen, a siren for summer sounds and busy feet.

"In the early days, we had unmanned microwave 'hops' to a transmitter in Pitman [N.J.]," said technician Hurst. "If the wind blew too hard, we got snow [on the screen]." Ratings never suffered, however, because whichever television channel broadcast the show (there were five of them during the two decades) had a large viewership.

The show seemed to be a career capper. But in 1981, after a three-

*The face may have changed
(a little), but the voice
remains the same.*
PHOTOGRAPH COURTESY OF
THE *COURIER-POST*

year recess from regular broadcasting, Hurst received an invitation. Radio station WPEN was restoring its old format and wanted him (and former partner Joe Grady) back for a two-week reunion to boost the station's bid for more listeners. As it turned out, there was one problem: Two weeks were not enough. Not nearly enough. Sacks of mail arrived at WPEN's front door. Television stations covered the story on the news. Perry Como called. So did Rosemary Clooney. Steve Lawrence. All the old singing stars. The old friends.

Grady and Hurst were back.

"It became an event," said Hurst.

They stayed on, joining revivified DJs such as Joe Niagra, and WPEN reclaimed its former luster (not to mention advertising revenue). The studio audience returned. The good music returned.

Grady retired in 1987, but Ed Hurst was "not about to retire." He was still there with the new century, hosting the latter-day "Steel Pier Radio Show" and "950 Club" on weekend afternoons. The studio audience was now in the realm of the imagination. So were the waves lapping the pier's barnacled limbs, above which the youthful—then middle-aged—announcer spun LPs and 45s on turntables. Truth is, Ed

Hurst's modern-day sounds were transmitted from a high-tech vault. But the classic recordings were smooth as ever, and the announcer's voice reassuringly unpretentious.

Once again, it was summertime at the pier.

The Atlantic City Pop Festival

It was a sunny Friday morning as the offbeat collection of vehicles inched its way down the Black Horse Pike. There were hearses, buses, U-Haul trucks, and flower-powered station wagons from as far away as Ontario and California, all with the same destination: the Atlantic City Race Course in Hamilton Township. The date was August 1, 1969. The three-day Atlantic City Pop Festival would kick off that afternoon.

That weekend, drumbeats would replace hoofbeats as more than two dozen acts representing the cream of contemporary rock 'n' roll, folk, soul, and blues would perform. The anticipation of the young crowd would be matched by equal feelings of fear and loathing by merchants in and around Atlantic City.

"These kids, who are repulsive to 95 percent of the respectable people, will be coming in without leaving twenty cents behind, unless, of course, they buy a hot dog and some pot," complained George Hamid, owner of the Steel Pier.

Another merchant, incensed at the intrusion of the youthful counterculture at the racetrack, suggested the words "Atlantic City" be deleted from the name since the festival would tarnish the image of the region as a family resort.

Taking their cue from the merchants, authorities braced for the worst. More than two hundred state troopers were stationed at nearby Oakcrest High School. Police officers in Pleasantville and Atlantic City worked twelve-hour shifts for the festival's duration. Officers in Hamilton, Galloway, Egg Harbor Township, and Egg Harbor City were placed on twenty-four-hour call. As part of the festival surveillance, state police took more than four hundred photographs and shot more than twenty-five hundred feet of movie footage. Augmenting the police were one hundred private security guards on the racecourse grounds.

*Booker T. & the M.G.'s (from left, Donald "Duck" Dunn, Booker T. Jones,
Steve Cropper, and Al Jackson Jr.), best known for such hits as "Green Onions" and
"Time Is Tight," brought their brand of soul music to the Atlantic City Pop Festival
in August 1969.*

PHOTOGRAPH COURTESY OF THE *COURIER-POST*

Festival organizers had a more optimistic view. The event was the brainchild of the Electric Factory, Philadelphia's premier rock 'n' roll venue, which had its share of run-ins with then–Police Commissioner Frank Rizzo. Festival producers—Herb, Alan, and Jerry Spivak, Shelley Kaplan, and Larry Magid—envisioned an event that would provide top-flight music in a relaxed, outdoor atmosphere. All they lacked was a site.

Herb Spivak had attended the Miami Pop Festival earlier in the year and believed the Jersey Shore, with its youthful, summertime population, would be a prime spot for a rock festival. Ocean City and other resorts turned down the opportunity to host the event. At the last minute, the racecourse management stepped in and offered the use of the five hundred–acre facility for a hundred thousand dollars. It was a calculated risk; the festival would end only five days before the start of the thoroughbred racing season on August 8.

Rock festivals had blossomed in popularity following the success of the 1967 Monterey Pop Festival in California. The Atlantic City Pop Festival marked the first rock festival in the East, staged two weeks before its more famous counterpart at Woodstock.

Despite all the concern surrounding the festival, the Atlantic City area was no stranger to rock concerts. The Beatles had performed at Convention Hall on August 30, 1964, and the Rolling Stones played at Steel Pier on July 1, 1966. However, the pop festival broke ground with its concentration of talent—more than two dozen bands and performers were onstage over a three-day period. It would be the equivalent of a summer's worth of Steel Pier shows in one weekend.

Promoters had lined up an impressive range of talent ranging from A (The American Dream) to Z (Frank Zappa). Established superstars like the Byrds and Jefferson Airplane were joined by such rising stars as Joni Mitchell, Creedence Clearwater Revival, and Janis Joplin. Also on the bill were blues legend B.B. King, soul music stars Booker T. and the M.G.'s, and 1950s rock 'n' roll wild man Little Richard. Promoters spent more than $150,000 on the performers' fees, including $30,000 for Joplin's seventy-five-minute performance. Tickets for the festival cost $6 per day or $15 for all three days.

The event went beyond music, with merchants catering to the youthful crowds. Set up near the two-dollar ticket window were double rows of vendors selling such items as leather goods, candles, incense, sandals, beaded belts and sashes, underground comics, books, and guitars.

Wooded sites for camping around the racecourse were available to festivalgoers planning to stay all three days. Others would stay at nearby campgrounds or drive the fourteen miles to Atlantic City and sleep on the beach.

The influx of young people made for an anything-goes attitude. During a Saturday afternoon performance by the Byrds, hundreds of fans stormed gates surrounding the track to get to the stage. Others seeking a better view clambered up seventy-five-foot light towers or a judge's reviewing stand. Less adventuresome fans retreated to the cashiers' windows inside the clubhouse and watched on closed-circuit television.

Temperature in the mid-eighties melted away inhibitions. Some fans could not resist the lure of the goose pond in the track's infield and stripped down for a swim. To avoid further incident, the track used its mobile sprinkling system to cool patrons.

While alcohol was not sold at the festival, alcohol and drugs were not difficult to find. Marijuana and LSD were the drugs of choice. State police arrested twenty people, but refrained from making more arrests because of possible reprisals from the crowd.

In the biggest breakdown of order, a small group of concertgoers ransacked the merchants' area early Sunday and stole about twenty thousand dollars worth of musical instruments, albums, and related merchandise.

Ultimately, the musicians were the glue that kept the festival together. A first-rate performance by Procol Harum got the event off to a strong start. The biggest disappointment of the festival also occurred on the first day, when folk singer Joni Mitchell walked off the stage midway through the fourth song of her set. She believed the crowd was not listening as she played the same verse twice without any reaction from the crowd. "I'm sorry. I can't play anymore," she said.

Any lingering disappointment from Mitchell's set was wiped away by Saturday's bands. Creedence Clearwater Revival, riding a wave of hits that included "Proud Mary" and "Green River," electrified the crowd during a forty-five-minute set Saturday night. Its San Francisco counterpart, Jefferson Airplane, closed the festival's second day with its hits "Somebody to Love" and "Volunteers."

Creedence Clearwater Revival (from left, Tom Fogerty, Doug Clifford, Stu Cook, and John Fogerty) performed their Top 5 hits "Proud Mary" and "Green River" at the Atlantic City Pop Festival.
PHOTOGRAPH COURTESY OF THE *COURIER-POST*

The momentum from Saturday's show carried over to Sunday, despite a steady rain that turned the track into mud. Janis Joplin whipped the crowd into a frenzy with her versions of "Ball and Chain" and "Down on Me." It was left to Little Richard to close the festivities, and he sent the crowd home happy with a sampling of his fifties hits, including "Lucille" and "Ready Teddy."

Final tallies for the festival were impressive, one hundred and eleven thousand fans over three days, including a track record of fifty thousand on Saturday. More than seventy-five thousand hot dogs and a hundred thousand cold drinks were sold.

The final chord had barely faded when debate over the festival and the use of drugs began. A headline in the *Philadelphia Inquirer* on August 5 blared "Mass Drug Orgy Charged at 3-Day Rock Festival." Hamilton Township Mayor William Davies said he and the township committee were "very much disappointed with the Racing Association for sponsoring such a disgraceful enclave."

Although some merchants reported no problems with the huge crowds, the township committee had its way and no more pop festivals were held at the racecourse. It was five years before another rock concert was held there, when Crosby, Stills, Nash, and Young performed on August 9, 1974.

In retrospect, the festival went off more smoothly that similar events in 1969. In April, extensive rioting broke out at a rock festival in Palm Springs, California, resulting in two hundred and fifty arrests. A festival in Denver ended abruptly with police releasing tear gas into the crowd.

Even though the Shore festival was the sixth largest of the decade, its fate was to be overshadowed by the festival held in upstate New York two weeks later. A successful documentary film and two soundtrack albums ensured Woodstock's place as the dominant festival of the decade. For those who attended the Atlantic City Pop Festival, undocumented on film or record, memories were all that remained. However, festivalgoers had the satisfaction of being at the center of the rock 'n' roll universe for one weekend in the summer of 1969.

The King of Marvin Gardens

Sitting, staring ahead intently, a bespectacled man in partial shadow collects his thoughts and leans forward to speak: "I promised I would tell you why I never eat fish." It's Jack Nicholson as David Staebler in the opening scene of the 1972 film *The King of Marvin Gardens*. For the next three minutes, Nicholson, playing a Philadelphia disk jockey, delivers a spellbinding monologue as he plays a character unlike any other in his more than forty-year acting career.

Released in the autumn of 1972, *The King of Marvin Gardens* now serves as a cinematic time capsule of Atlantic City shortly before casino gambling forever changed the landscape. Directed by Bob Rafelson, who received an Oscar nomination for *Five Easy Pieces*, the movie reunited him with Nicholson, a Best Actor nominee for *Five Easy Pieces*.

Rafelson assembled a strong cast for *The King of Marvin Gardens*, including Bruce Dern, who plays Jason Staebler, a con man and schemer who persuades his brother to leave Philadelphia for Atlantic City. "Get you ass down here. Our kingdom has come," he tells David in an early scene. Jason is pursuing a dream of going to Tiki, an island off the coast of Honolulu, and turning it into a haven for tourists. He envisions this kingdom as a way of escaping the gambling debts he owes to Lewis, a powerful local loan shark played by Scatman Crothers.

Nicholson plays the reclusive, withdrawn brother, at ease only when he is before a radio microphone. David Staebler struggles to keep up, both emotionally and physically, with his raucous sibling. The seething explosiveness that Nicholson brought to such films as *One Flew Over the Cuckoo Nest, The Shining,* and *Batman* is nowhere to be found in *The King of Marvin Gardens.*

Rounding out the cast is Ellen Burstyn as Sally, an aging girlfriend of Jason's. During an argument with David, Jason proposes that they leave Sally behind in Atlantic City when they go to Hawaii. In hysterics, she shoots and kills Jason, which sets the stage for David's riveting monologue (and one of Nicholson's finest scenes), when he sums up his loss for his radio listeners.

The post–Labor Day Atlantic City—the movie was filmed there and in Ventnor, Margate, and Philadelphia between October 1971 and January 1972—provides a rich backdrop for the film as the high hopes of summer fade into the bleak reality of winter.

"Atlantic City in the off-season was slightly seedy and had a certain charm," explained Jacob Brackman, the screenwriter for *The King of Marvin Gardens.* Brackman lived in Atlantic City between 1948 and 1953, from age five to ten, and returned in 1971 to do research for the script.

"Atlantic City became a character in the film," said Brackman, who drew on his childhood memories when writing the script. "My aunt was a shill who used to dress up like a tourist and bid up the price at a boardwalk auction." Brackman incorporated that piece of family history into a scene on the boardwalk involving the audition of auctioneers attended by the Staeblers.

Other Atlantic City traditions and Shore landmarks are used to good effect in the movie. The Marlborough-Blenheim Hotel—renamed the Essex Carlton for the movie—serves as the base of operation for the

Actor Jack Nicholson portrayed David Staebler in The King of Marvin Gardens.
PHOTOGRAPH COURTESY OF THE *COURIER-POST*

Actor Bruce Dern portrayed Jason Staebler in The King of Marvin Gardens.
PHOTOGRAPH COURTESY OF THE *COURIER-POST*

Staeblers. Jason tells his brother it offers the "finest accommodations on the boardwalk. Woodrow Wilson used to stay here." Captain Starn's Restaurant and Yacht Bar is the setting for a key meeting between the brothers and two Japanese entrepreneurs.

The movie also shows that gambling did not begin with the first legalized casino in 1978. Signs for Banko and Pokerino, games of chance, are shown on the boardwalk. A line of dialogue also foreshadows what Atlantic City will become. During a discussion of business in Tiki, Jason Staebler tells his brother: "The casino is the name of the game. It's where you rise or fall."

Despite the downbeat nature of the film, Brackman recalls the set as a happy one. The cast and crew stayed at the Howard Johnson Motor Lodge and was visible in the community. Dern, an avid runner, could be seen jogging each morning on the boardwalk.

The King of Marvin Gardens was a homecoming of sorts for Nicholson, too. He grew up in Monmouth County and many family members and friends came to Atlantic City for a reunion. Following his breakthrough performances in *Easy Rider* and *Five Easy Pieces*, Nicholson was on the verge of movie stardom when he agreed to do *The King of Marvin Gardens*.

"For me, it's a movie where I got to play something that I would normally never get to play. That's what my pleasure in the film is," he told *Crawdaddy!* magazine in an interview published in the February 1973 issue. "It's such an underdrawn and withdrawn character that it's not going to add anything to public magnetism as far as I'm concerned," he added.

The movie was originally titled *The Philosopher King*, a reference to David Staebler's intellectual side. It was retitled *The King of Atlantic City*, but Rafelson finally settled on *The King of Marvin Gardens*, because it was less specific but inspired memories of Atlantic City through its association with the board game Monopoly. One scene filmed for the movie included the title phrase but was edited out of the final version.

In his *Crawdaddy!* interview, Nicholson summed up *The King of Marvin Gardens* this way: "It's strong and different and has a lot of artistic courage, but it's not going to draw."

Nicholson proved correct in his analysis. Made for a million dollars, the movie did not make a profit in its initial release. It made the Top 10 lists of several film critics and quietly slipped out of circulation and was rarely shown on television. It was not released on video until 1993.

The passing years have not diminished its achievements. *The Time Out Film Guide* (fourth edition, 1995) calls it "one of the most underrated films of the decade." Nicholson still speaks highly of the movie and *The King of Marvin Gardens* remains a cinematic treasure waiting to be discovered in the video store.

FAMOUS/INFAMOUS EVENTS✦

Tale of the Timbers

The timbers lie like ordered driftwood, suggesting the contours of a boat and bearing the splinters of a mystery. Housed in a roofless pavilion, they are a skeleton within a skeleton aside a quiet intersection in Cape May Point, the state's southernmost locale and one of its richer repositories of grounded ships and maritime lore. What the air hasn't rotted, termites have eaten; yet this crumbling vestige still fascinates. Fronting the wreck and blanched by the years, an engraving on a stone pedestal identifies the remains as those of the "British Sloop of War *Martin*," presumably done in by an offshore engagement during the War of 1812.

Official records and letters say otherwise. It takes neither sleuth nor seafarer to determine that what we have here . . . is the wrong body. This body was exhumed from the Cape May Point beach nearly five decades ago after dozing beneath the sands for at least 141 years. The faded engraving to the contrary, its identity is uncertain.

His Majesty's sloop *Martin* did patrol these waters during the summer of 1813, when James Madison was in the White House (torched by the British the following year), and the Delaware Bay provided strategic access to both Philadelphia and Washington. On July 28, HMS *Martin* sunk the U.S. privateer *Snapdragon* and sent her crew ashore. The tide went out, and the *Martin* came aground on Crow's Shoal off the coast of Cape May Point on the bay side.

The next morning, word of the *Snapdragon*'s demise reached U.S. Commander Samuel Angus and his Delaware flotilla poised at Dennis Creek, which fed the bay a dozen miles to the north. Angus promptly brought eight gunboats down the bay and encountered the immobilized *Martin*. The stage was set for fireworks.

The *Martin*'s cannonade was long; the flotilla's lacked firepower. Still, the *Martin* was sustaining some damage when one of the U.S. gunboats drifted from the line and into trouble. The *Martin* and nearby British frigate *Junon* (similarly hamstrung by shallow water) dispatched eight small boats packed with men and weapons to target the American stray (known as gunboat 121).

Angus would later say he didn't order the other American gunboats to aid 121 because the priority remained the *Martin*. Isolated and under siege, 121 fired three rounds of grapeshot at the attacking British boats before its long gun came unhinged. The Brits suffered losses (eleven dead) but overwhelmed the Americans and forced surrender. Gunboat 121, its "upper works materially injured," was towed away by its tormentors, but not before they stripped the masts and helped themselves to a bit of plunder if not bloodlust. Seven wounded mates of 121 were likely treated and put ashore.

The skirmish and its aftermath are detailed in a series of letters written by Angus; his superior, Commodore Alexander Murray; and Sailing Master William W. Sheed, who commanded gunboat 121. Sheed claimed that a "strong ebb tide" had swept away his boat, and extolled the bravery of his crew (and indirectly himself). Angus and Murray pointed fingers at each other—Murray disdainful of Angus's failure to assist 121, Angus blaming substandard guns and gunpowder and calling Murray's stewardship "shameful." The squabble found its way to Secretary of the Navy William Jones and an eventual court of inquiry that cited Angus for "errors in judgment."

This official correspondence, published in the book *The Naval War of 1812: A Documentary History*, negates the *Martin* myth. A letter from Sheed to Angus dated August 6, 1813, finds the captured 121 commander on board HMS *Martin* "off Providence, Rhode Island." For a sunken ship, ol' *Martin* had pretty strong sea legs.

It was seaworthy enough, in fact, to stay afloat another four years. According to the official "Ships of the Royal Navy" listing, the thirty by one hundred–foot "*Martin* Sloop 18," built in Bermuda in 1809, perished off the west coast of Ireland on August 12, 1817. It is one of a dozen *Martins* on the Royal list, but the only one that existed during the relevant time period. So, whatever ship bones rest in the weeds at Lighthouse and Coral avenues, they don't belong to any HMS *Martin*.

Hanging on the wall in Cape May Point Mayor Malcolm Fraser's office in the new borough hall are copies of two watercolors that depict the *Martin*'s clashes with the *Snapdragon* and Delaware flotilla. Painted sometime in the second half of the nineteenth century, the paintings show guns blazing amid a display of colors: the Union Jack versus the Stars and Stripes.

"We know there was a battle," said Fraser. "And now we know that boat is not the *Martin*."

Indeed, the dimensions of the landed skeleton approximate not the *Martin*, but ill-fated gunboat 121 of the so-called "Jeffersonian Gunboat Navy," wrangled by tall Tom from a stingy Congress. Built in 1808 at the Philadelphia Naval Shipyard, gunboat 121 was fifty feet long and seventeen-and-a-half feet across its beam.

But the ship bones may not belong to 121, either. A few years ago, a museum curator of archaeology pointed to the "size of the hull timbers" and the presence of "hexagonal wood trunnels (fasteners)" as evidence that the Cape May Point remains are not those of 121, but of, perhaps, a merchantman from the mid-eighteenth century.

Whatever its origins, the mystery boat was exposed by a 1954 storm, after time and tide had buried it in sand. That same year, according to Fraser, local developer George Pettinos extracted the husk from the beach as he was installing Cape May Point's first jetty. Pettinos moved the shipwreck to its current site, land now owned by his estate.

According to local oral history, two cannonballs surfaced with the boat hull and were given to a man (now deceased) who lived across from town hall. Since British rounds of the day typically were marked, the cannonballs could be a key piece of the puzzle. Gunboat 121? A merchantman from the eighteenth century? Some other poor vessel sandbagged by shallow water or assaulted on the seas?

Fraser was rooting for 121: "It would be the only Jeffersonian gunboat extant," he said.

Has anyone seen a pair of cannonballs?

Woodbury's Rebel General

Vengeance was in the air and the demand for it seemed to increase with each footstep as the mob of angry residents marched down Broad Street in Woodbury.

It was 1863 and the United States was bitterly divided by the Civil War, the bloodiest conflict in the nation's history. However, the mob was united in its quest—the destruction of the summer home of Samuel Gibbs French. Such an action would have been unthinkable a decade earlier when French fought heroically in the Mexican War and was honored by New Jersey for his achievements.

All of that was far from the thoughts of the mob as is drew closer to French's home at the southeast corner of Broad Street and Aberdeen Place. After the Mexican War ended, French met and married E. Matilda Symington of Mississippi in 1853 and purchased a plantation near Greenville, Mississippi. He retired from the army in 1856, intending to work on his plantation. The Gloucester County native maintained his ties to South Jersey and purchased a summer home in Woodbury.

With the election of Abraham Lincoln as president in 1860, the threat of secession became a reality. Eleven southern states, including Mississippi, chose to leave the Union. As the threat of war loomed, French faced an agonizing choice: Should he fight for the North or the South?

French cast his lot with the rebels and explained his decision this way. "A man cannot choose his birthplace, but he can choose his residence. For me, I prefer the South."

The mob chose to send a message to French after learning of his decision to fight for the Confederacy through an article in a local newspaper. With French thousands of miles away, his vacant house because a convenient target for the mob's wrath.

"Down with the rebel! Hang him!" the crowd cried as it arrived at his two-story, yellow-brick home. French's one-time neighbors now regarded him as an enemy of the people. The Confederate general was hanged in effigy, and the mob stormed the house, intending to burn it to the ground. Items from the house were thrown out into the street. Joseph Carter, a quick-thinking sheriff, moved to defuse the crowd's white-hot emotions. He managed to climb to an upper window above the crowd and unfurl an American flag.

The sight of the flag, the proud symbol of the states that remained in the union, had a soothing effect on the crowd, which stopped its attack and slowly began to disperse. Carter's fast thinking had saved French's house. It would be up to French to restore his reputation.

French began life in Mullica Hill, Gloucester County, on November 22, 1818, one of seven children of Samuel and Rebecca French. Determination and discipline marked the boy from an early age.

His decision to join the military was made when he was eight years old, after seeing a portrait of a soldier in uniform in a Philadelphia store. The storekeeper befriended the young French and told him the portrait was of his son, who was attending the U.S. Military Academy at West Point in New York; French set the goal of attending West Point.

He realized that ambition, earning an appointment to West Point in 1839. Among his classmates was Ulysses Grant, a future opponent on the battlefield and president of the United States.

After graduating fourteenth in a class of thirty-nine, French was commissioned a brevet second lieutenant and assigned to Fort Macon, North Carolina. A year later, French became an eyewitness to history when he was invited by inventor Samuel F. B. Morse to watch the transmission of the first telegraph message from Washington, D.C., to Baltimore, the site of the 1844 Democratic National Convention.

French made his mark in the army during the Mexican War between 1846 and 1848. Serving under General Zachary Taylor, the future twelfth president, French was cited by the general for "gallant and meritorious conduct" in fighting at Monterey. During one battle, French's horse was shot out from underneath him. In February 1847, he was severely wounded in the leg during the Battle of Buena Vista. Thanks to his battlefield achievements, French's rank during the war rose from lieutenant to captain. After the war, French was honored for his service by the New Jersey Legislature and presented with a ceremonial sword.

Following his 1853 marriage, French settled in Mississippi and tended to agricultural matters. He visited Woodbury during the summer in the years before the Civil War and began to raise his family. Tragedy

Two Wars *was republished in 1999 by Blue Acorn Press. The cover photograph of Samuel Gibbs French was taken during his Civil War service.*

PHOTOGRAPH BY ELIZABETH WILK

struck in 1857 when his wife died while giving birth to the couple's second child, a son.

His ties to the South grew stronger, and when the War between the States broke out, French sided with his adopted state of Mississippi. A surviving photograph of French during the Civil War shows a stern-looking man with a handlebar mustache and receding hairline, his military uniform reflecting his determination that he was following the right course.

Because of French's military experience, the governor of Mississippi appointed him a lieutenant colonel and chief of ordnance in acquiring arms and gunpowder for the state. By October 1861, Jefferson Davis, the president of the Confederacy, made French a brigadier general. A year later came a promotion to major general.

From Mississippi, French traveled north and helped to fortify Wilmington, North Carolina, and Petersburg, Virginia. The fortifications he helped to construct in Petersburg withstood Union attacks until April 1865, shortly before General Robert E. Lee surrendered the Confederate forces under his command.

In May 1863, French was assigned to the Army of Tennessee under General Joseph Johnston. French fought in the Atlanta and Tennessee campaigns and the battles of Kennesaw Mountain and Nashville in 1864. During the last part of the war, he was almost blind because of an eye infection. By the war's end in 1865, he was on inactive service in Mobile, Alabama.

After the showdown at his northern home in Woodbury, the property was confiscated and sold by the U.S. government. His plantation in Mississippi suffered from the ravages of war. In *Two Wars*, his autobiography, which was published in 1901, French wrote movingly of the desolate scene he found when he returned to his southern home: "Fences burned; bridges destroyed; a forest of tall weeds. Horses, mules, cattle, sheep, poultry, and implements of every kind all gone; wealth, servants, comforts—all means of support for my family gone, all lost save honor."

Because the plantation was overrun, French sent his family, including his mother, sister, and new wife, Mary Fontaine-Abercrombie, to

56

SAMUEL G. FRENCH.

Samuel Gibbs French is shown in his early eighties. This photograph appeared in Two Wars, *his autobiography, which was published in 1901.*

PHOTOGRAPH BY TOM WILK

live in Woodbury after the war ended. Unaware their home had been confiscated, the women were treated as pariahs. The baggage handlers at the Woodbury train station refused to handle their belongings. Finally, a Quaker came forward and took the women into his home.

A pair of northern cousins, Clayton and Samuel H. French, were instrumental in helping French get back on his feet. The cousins helped French reacquire his Woodbury home and rebuild his Mississippi plantation. French was pardoned by General Grant, his West Point classmate, and declared himself "loyal to the Constitution and rights of the United States" and gradually had a reconciliation with his northern neighbors.

After the death of his second wife, French returned to live in Woodbury during the summer to avoid the hotter temperatures in the South. French's patriotism was still in evidence at age seventy-nine when he volunteered to serve in the Spanish-American War in 1898. President McKinley turned him down.

French died on April 20, 1910, at the age of ninety-one in Florala, Alabama. It marked the end of a remarkable life. He grew up hearing firsthand accounts of life in the American Revolution and lived long enough to see the invention of the airplane and baseball's World Series. Symbolic of his divided loyalties in life, he was wrapped in the American and Confederate flags in his casket when he was laid to rest in St. John's Cemetery in Pensacola, Florida.

The Wildwood Boardwalk

They came under cover of darkness. Moonlight flitted through inky clouds whose swiftness outflanked the men fanning out below. Armed with heavy-duty hammers and official sanction, the night brigade went to work.

It was 12:01 A.M. on a Sunday morning in 1920, and the timeless ocean's muffled roar accompanied the sound of splintering wood. The marching orders were to dismantle an eight-block stretch of the Wildwood boardwalk. City Commissioner Oliver Bright led the nocturnal charge cannily planned to elude the long arm of the law—local judges didn't work on Sunday, so there would be no cease-and-desist order.

The wrecking crew banged away; the boardwalk decking yielded. By sunrise, it had been picked clean.

The demolition was inspired by a mix of civic pragmatism and personal motive. Commissioner Bright's bailiwick was finance, and he sought to bolster sagging city coffers by pushing the boardwalk oceanward and spawning a new generation of taxable lots. But the public servant was also a real estate professional who welcomed an expansion of the Wildwood portfolio. A new boardwalk construction project had been stalled by squabbles with local merchants and related legal proceedings. The Bright initiative, in effect, forced everyone's hand. For the Wildwood boardwalk, it would be a crucial link in an unpredictable evolution.

"I can't help but think that dad had some self-interest—it was a big plum to him," said Bob Bright Sr., who, as an eleven-year-old, joined his father the commissioner on that long-ago demolition date, Boy Scout hatchet in hand. "But also, Wildwood was strapped [for cash]."

By the end of World War I, the Wildwood boardwalk needed a facelift. Funds were limited, but the city finally approved and began a boardwalk project—not just the replacement of rotting boards, but construction of a whole new walk closer to the ocean, from Cedar Avenue to Montgomery Avenue, with a sizable section connecting with the existing boardwalk to the south.

The project drew opponents, however, including prominent merchant Gilbert Blaker, the rolling-chair impresario and theater operator who leased Excursion Pavilion on the boardwalk near the foot of Cedar Avenue. Blaker protested that the city had assured him that the boardwalk would not be moved for a few years, and took legal action that halted construction. For the time being.

The impetus for boardwalk relocation was Wildwood's ever expanding beach. It was not a new phenomenon. The coastline's mysterious littoral drift had long been exporting sands from the north, and Five Mile Beach—encompassing all the Wildwoods—came closer each year to shaking hands with the horizon. Decades later, eyeing Atlantic City's narrowing strand, people would say, "Atlantic City's beach is in Wildwood"—not technically correct, but a strong image.

Workers fashion a new stretch of the Wildwood boardwalk in May 1939.
PHOTOGRAPH COURTESY OF THE *COURIER-POST*

Indeed, the enduring portrait of Wildwood is a seashore town on the move: its beach, its great amusement rides spinning skyward, its frenetic Midway, its energetic visitors combing the thrillscape. And its boardwalk. Rudimentary walkways began appearing in these parts in 1890, as shopkeepers and hoteliers erected portable structures that could be removed and stored during the winter. By the turn of the century, the resort's increased foot traffic convinced municipal leaders to spring for a boardwalk along Atlantic Avenue; in 1904, the Borough of Wildwood went one better, building an elevated boardwalk east of Atlantic, closer to the ocean.

Soon after, North Wildwood and Holly Beach, the latter a borough south of Wildwood, built boardwalks that linked with Wildwood's, giving the island a continuous, two-and-a-half mile promenade.

With new Ocean Pier creasing the Wildwood surf, the resort was ready to challenge Atlantic City for summer tourists. Stores, eateries, and amusements surfaced on the boards. Blaker's rolling chairs debuted and, as the immutable ocean lapped the sands, a new generation of visitors negotiated the boardwalk. But the beach continued to swell, and in 1911, the borough council authorized construction of a new boardwalk from Cedar Avenue to the Wildwood northern border at 26th Street—closer to the ocean, of course.

The following year, the boroughs of Wildwood and Holly Beach merged to form the City of Wildwood. Which brings us to the nighttime raid of 1920. With a crucial portion of the boardwalk stripped, Blaker and the business community relented, allowing the city to proceed with its plans to relocate the great wooden way. By August 1921, city crews had completed a new, oceanward boardwalk connected to its predecessor by a right-angled spur at Montgomery Avenue. Commissioner Bright, though, lost his job. Still smarting over his boldness, boardwalk business owners had triggered a successful recall vote.

A few years later, an infestation of worms undermined the cedar pilings of the Wildwood boardwalk's northern leg, and in 1925, a new spruce walk with concrete pilings rose along that stretch. Two years later, the city's southernmost section of boardwalk was completed from Montgomery to the border of Wildwood Crest.

In the ensuing years, rescue and repair crews would battle fires, hurricanes, a stray lion, and a few stray humans, but the boardwalk remained the gateway to Wildwood's robust entertainment. The Big Bands played here, as did Ellington and a host of additional marquee names. Animal acts were surefire attractions until an unfortunate episode in 1938 when Tuffy the Lion broke loose, joined the boardwalk crowd, and killed a man.

The restrictions of World War II dimmed the boardwalk dazzle, and the Hurricane of '44 wreaked havoc, but the 1950s ushered in a new era of seashore fun stoked by trams, teenage record hops, and more daring and diverse amusement rides offered by the likes of Hunt's Pier and Marine Pier.

Indeed, the Wildwood boardwalk, a stationary swath of wooden planks, has been for decades a conduit for perpetual motion and vertiginous excitement. During the high season, it is the stage for ten thousand daily dramas played out in nooks and crannies, at the sirenlike game booths and on the oversize piers, where great wheels revolve against the sky and breathless roller coasters test riders' nerves and stomachs. On a torrid August afternoon, the sun paints fire on your forehead, and the throttle is full open on Morey's Piers, where brave patrons dangle from long chains that swing about an axle, or scream in ecstatic dizziness in inverted seats on a careening coaster.

Elsewhere on the boards, movement is grounded but no less intoxicating. This is the terrain of the barker, the intersection of crafty shots and well-crafted pitches. The irresistible sheen of the gaming stand invites you to aim, toss, squirt, or shoot for the bull's-eye . . . and keep your eyes on the prize. For contestants ranging from tots to octogenarians, the game's the thing.

Near the boards, another body remains in a dynamic state in Wildwood: the beach. It continues to grow, now extending nearly a half-mile to water's edge, with virtually unlimited seats for marbles tournaments, sailboat races, and concerts-by-the-sea.

The boardwalk, however, has stayed put since the twenties. A makeshift, piecemeal affair a century ago, it became a solid link across time, tastes, and community boundaries. Now, new blood and fresh enterprises are promising a pathway to the future.

The route has been altered more than once, but the destination remains constant. Boardwalk business owners may have ousted Commissioner Oliver Bright from office in 1921, but like Supreme Court justices, the boardwalk has its job for life.

Surf and Turf

The desk clerk was sweating. The three men who stood before him wore their menace like a custom-made shirt. He wasn't used to dealing with this sort. They had affixed their names to the register—Max Hoff and Charles Schwartz from Philadelphia, Abe Bernstein from Detroit—and now they leaned on the hotel counter and waited.

The clerk cleared his throat and fidgeted like a pigeon on the boardwalk. "Excuse me," he said in a voice lodged somewhere between his tonsils and his sinuses. With that, he turned on his heel and disappeared through a door.

A moment later, the manager strode forward, glanced at the register, and appraised his would-be patrons. His words fell with icy politeness: "I'm sorry, we have no vacancies at this time."

Another voice—angry and unhinged—promptly blasted through the lobby. "What the hell is this?" screamed the burly man with the olive complexion and ridge of white scar tissue on his left cheek. Somewhat short on finesse, he proceeded to remove a small oil canvas from the wall and smash it on a Chippendale table. The manager reached for the telephone.

The rebuffed Hoff, Schwartz, and Bernstein and their overzealous defender were quickly hustled out of the hotel—but not by the authorities. These underworld kingpins had journeyed to Atlantic City for a convention not likely to be touted by any chamber of commerce, but fortunately for them, the local police were on the payroll. The volatile scarface was none other than Alphonse Capone and, in this instance, his anger had the high moral ground. The hotel was restricted all right—not against gangsters, but Jews.

The man who delivered Al Capone and his Jewish brethren was Atlantic City's big boss himself, Enoch J. "Nucky" Johnson. Tuning out the irate Capone, he drove the four to his posh digs at the Ritz-Carlton where they were joined by a lineup of gangland all-stars from New Orleans, Cleveland, Kansas City, Boston, Newark, and, of course, New York. The Irish, Italians, Sicilians, Jews, and Slavs assembled for organized crime's equal-opportunity summit of May 13–16, 1929.

Capone's turf was Chicago, and New York's already legendary Charles "Lucky" Luciano, Frank Costello, Meyer Lansky, and "Dutch" Schultz were putting aside their own squabbles to stand united against the midwestern mobster whose violent ways, they figured, were hurting their industry. The avowed goal of the conference was to cool everyone's jets and establish a commission to arbitrate disputes. But the fine print called for the neutering of Capone.

The Brooklyn-born Capone had been bucking an even more threatening storm back home in the Windy City. Although his syndicate controlled Chicago's extortion rackets and claimed a healthy share of the bootlegging trade, the North Side gang led by "Bugs" Moran had been muscling in. Moran's men hijacked liquor shipments, burned down a dog track, and turned selected Capone henchmen into target boards.

Capone retaliated with a cascade of violence that stunned even fellow crime lords. On the frigid morning of February 14, 1929, a stolen squad car pulled up to a Chicago garage, and four men—two wearing police uniforms—got out. Inside, seven of Moran's workforce awaited delivery of a load of hooch. The two "officers" entered the garage, shouted the familiar "raid," confiscated weapons, and lined up the unlucky seven with their faces to a brick wall. The other two raiders then stepped forward, machine guns at the ready. The fusillade lasted only seconds and was soon memorialized as the St. Valentine's Day Massacre.

Less than three months later, on May 7, Capone invited a hundred close associates to a banquet for three of his top operatives. Wine and brandy flowed; toasts abounded. Late in the night, Capone changed the mood. He brandished a baseball bat and bludgeoned the guests of honor, two of whom had been the shooters on St. Valentine's Day. When batting practice was over, the men were shot and their bodies dumped on the highway.

A public outcry galvanized law enforcement and elected officials. Mob violence had reached an unacceptable level, even for the mobsters.

Atlantic City Director of Public Safety W. S. Cuthbert issued the order: "Pick up Al Capone if he is found and arrest him as an undesirable." But Nucky Johnson, who ran the city's political machine and presided over the seashore rackets, peddled his influence and backed it with cash. The out-of-town "delegates" checked into the Ritz-Carlton and carved out their futures.

It was a mild spring, and the salt air beckoned. Racketeers took to rolling chairs and discussed matters of blood and money on the breezy boardwalk. They took off their shoes and walked along the water's edge, envisioning a world where each chieftain could conduct business in his own domain without fear of rivals or reprisals. Exclusive territories. No bloodshed.

Afterward, Capone would falsely imply that the conference was his brainchild and say, "I'm tired of gang murders. . . . I spent the week in Atlantic City trying to make peace among the various gang leaders of my city. I have the word of each of these men that there will be no more shootings." Yet archenemy Moran had remained in Chicago, seething in the wake of St. Valentine's Day.

The likely architect of the conference was Frank Costello, a key member of the New York contingent bent on transferring power in Chicago to respected veteran gangster Johnny Torrio, who had been Capone's mentor. "There are two ways to power," said Torrio, who had the civilized look of a corporate department head. "A Capone can rule for awhile by blood and terror, but there will always be some who fight him with his own weapons. On the other hand, the man who can make money for others will eventually be regarded as indispensable." Capone, Torrio concluded, was now dispensable.

To the brain trust gathered in Atlantic City, Capone was a pariah. He was excluded from deliberations like a schoolboy dispatched from the classroom. He strolled the boards with a lone bodyguard and shipped a box of saltwater taffy to his wife, Mae, and ten-year-old son at their Prairie Avenue home in Chicago. One afternoon he supposedly bumped into Moses Annenberg, formerly a Hearst reporter in Chicago and no stranger to racketeers. "Can we get some publicity out of this, Moe?" asked Capone. "You can count on it," Annenberg replied.

For Capone, the news would be all bad. Word was filtered through a handpicked journalist from United Press, and it came out sanitary and self-serving for the conclave of criminals. The delegations had signed an agreement, wrote the reporter, that abolished assassination, compelled members to relinquish their machine guns, and created a commission headed by Torrio to resolve "controversies." Then came the blockbuster: Al Capone was to surrender the reins of his organization.

Doubtless the commission had plans for the millions of dollars generated annually by Capone's gambling, prostitution, protection, and bootlegging interests. But the Big Man was not in a surrendering mood. The Atlantic City conference had produced sweeping new guidelines, but the only way to enforce them was to violate them—that is, at the point of a gun. Capone was defiant, but decided to lay low for awhile. He went directly to Philadelphia, staged his own arrest for carrying a concealed weapon, and played the contrite hood. He could, however, still run matters from a jail cell (though the one-year sentence was a bit longer than anticipated), and his empire continued to flourish.

It would take an attack on his flanks to ground Capone for keeps. A dedicated trio of crime fighters launched an assault on the organization's books as well as its booze. U.S. Attorney George E. Q. Johnson, Treasury agent Eliot Ness, and IRS investigator Frank Wilson were smart and tenacious, and public opinion sat in their corner. Two years after the summit at the Shore, his brain already invaded by syphilis contracted years earlier, Al Capone was convicted of income tax evasion and sentenced to the federal penitentiary. He was three months shy of his thirty-third birthday, and though he would be released from prison in eight years, his time at the pinnacle had passed.

The Reluctant Miss America

There she was—but not for long.

Miss America accepted her crowning glory and felt the first tendrils of panic. This was not what she had figured. As the hour pressed toward midnight, seven thousand strong celebrated on the sweeping floorboards of the Steel Pier Marine Ballroom, where an art deco stage cast its glitter toward the Atlantic Ocean. Weighted down by his familiar green robe and foot-long white beard, King Neptune paid homage. Alex Bartha and the boys on the bandstand struck up "So Rare," a ballad that captured the cynosure of the evening—Bette Cooper—and the events to follow.

Later, in the calm and safety of the Lafayette Hotel, the newly minted beauty queen and her family commiserated. The simple pleasures of their home in Hackettstown beckoned. The next morning, as newsreel cameras bunched under an electric sign advertising "Come See Miss America 1937," the gathering crowd at Steel Pier awaited the winner, the runners-up, the crush of pageant and public officials, and the customary storm of flash bulbs. All showed, except one.

Miss America was AWOL; Bette had flown the coop.

At their hotel suite, Mr. and Mrs. LeBrun Cooper were noncommittal about their daughter's whereabouts. Neither the mayor nor the pageant director could pry loose answers. In the relative quiet of the bedroom, a reporter listened to a uniformed woman as she dusted a vanity. There was a "young man," she said, who had sent orchids to Bette every morning.

Frank Off had purchased the Brighton Hotel in 1923, two years before starting his nursery business in Linwood and years before becoming Atlantic City's finance commissioner. By the time his son, Lou, joined the operation, orchids held sway over roses and gardenias. The twenty-two-year-old Junior Off resided at his father's hotel and tooled a nine-hundred-dollar maroon Buick Special convertible daily to Brighton Farms. He had family standing, good looks, and self-assuredness—qualities prized by a financially strapped Miss America Pageant seeking volunteers for the 1937 spectacle. Any of the fifty-one contestants would look just fine on the arm of Lou Off.

They stepped from the "American Beauty Special" at Union Station and seized the spotlight. Their ranks included Miss Eastern Shore, Miss Miami, Miss Buckeye Lake, Miss West Chester County, the coy and the coquettish, the straightforward and the smalltownish. Their rush to judgment would take place in Atlantic City, where the marquees trumpeted silent screen Adonis Ramon Novarro in-person at the Million Dollar Pier, comedian Joe Lewis at the 500 Club, the Ice Follies slashing through the expansive Auditorium, and, at the Globe, Wanda the Dancer.

It was all too bright and brazen for a seventeen-year-old, apple-cheeked blonde from northwestern New Jersey. The nightly talent competition, luncheons at the big hotels, the press, the parades, the girls in their come-hither poses. Bette Cooper was partial to basketball, tennis, and churchgoing, and she still wasn't certain what she was doing here. That summer night on the islet in Lake Hopatcong, the air scented by steaming hot dogs, the roller coaster deafening and dangerous, her girlfriends had virtually shoved her before the beauty contest judges and—wonder of wonders—she had emerged as "Miss Bertrand Island" with a berth in the Miss America Pageant.

So the whole family came to Atlantic City for a week's vacation and, reluctantly, Bette joined the fray. She sang "When the Poppies Bloom Again" in a thin but engaging soprano, floated down the boardwalk before one hundred and sixty thousand parade watchers, donned a leopard-spot bathing suit, then a coral velvet, V-neck gown for the Friday night beauty ball. With attention-getters like Phyl Randall (Miss California) and her "kiss me again lips" on display, Bette gave herself no chance—nor did she aspire to the throne. Yet she was selected as "most beautiful" in evening gown and runner-up in the "charming personality" department, and suddenly, she was in the hunt.

On Saturday afternoon, the pageant took a breather in anticipation of that evening's final judging. Lou Off and Bette motored out of Atlantic City. She had caught a seashore cold early in the week and had been subsisting mainly on orange juice, and Off figured that Harry Styer's little seafood eatery in Somers Point would nourish his weakening charge. In addition, he had some food for thought.

"What if you win?" he asked.

Be careful what you wish, for it may come true. While Bette did not covet the crown, she was quite interested in the decisive, mature young man who had been appointed her "chauffeur." Later, her father would say that Off was "her first fancy and an awfully nice young fellow." But Off did not fancy the prospect of permanently tagging along with a Miss America, and he made his feelings clear.

It took three ballots for the judges to choose Bette Cooper over Miss Texas, a seventeen-year-old brunette, and a Miss North Carolina renowned for her tap-dancing. As the music swelled, so did Bette's headache. In the wings were a Persian lamb coat, a Hollywood screen test, and a hopscotch of personal appearances. She looked for her adviser, but Lou Off had made a hasty retreat.

At two A.M. the phone rang in Off's hotel apartment, and he listened to the sobs of a forlorn young woman. Outside, the multipaned windows of the Brighton Casino reflected the scattered lights on the boardwalk, and the hulking silhouette of the Traymore Hotel loomed to the north. Off fetched his Buick from the garage and sped to the Lafayette, where he parked at curbside and bounded through the arched entrance. Waiting in the foyer, LeBrun Cooper, a Warren County engineer, was grim. His wife did not want to "lose her baby," he said. They all wanted to go home. Off had the means and nerve to make that happen.

He returned at 4:30 with a muscular buddy who helped usher Bette down the fire escape and into the freedom of the early morning. Flanked by trolley tracks, they drove south on Atlantic Avenue to Margate as light began to thread the sky. Off turned onto Amherst Avenue, sighted the pilings, and parked head-on against the bulkhead. Tethered to the catwalk in the bay were a dozen boats, including a motorized Hubert-Johnson that would be a getaway skiff.

Exhausted, Bette ducked into the narrow cabin and fell asleep. Off fired up the Chrysler engine and headed for the eye of the uproar: Steel Pier. What better spot to avoid detection than right under the pageant's collective noses?

The plan was to outlast the daylight search-and-scramble, then drive Bette home under cover of night. Off had prepared well, bringing sandwiches and fishing gear for the excursion. He cast anchor and tossed in a line. As the consternation arose onshore, he leisurely trolled for blues. His portable radio conveyed the city's shocking news and an avowal from Director of Public Safety William Cuthbert: "If she's in this county, my boys will find her." Distanced from the tumult, Off and his drowsing passenger drifted with the tide.

After a half-day at sea, Off guided his cruiser back to Margate, where the trusty Buick was waiting. His comrade, George Pennington, accompanied Miss America and her official driver on the final, unsanctioned mission of the 1937 pageant. Seashore became countryside which gave way to mountains, as the trio hurried up the Black Horse Pike, then due north on Route 206 through Princeton and Somerville and, finally, to Hackettstown.

The three-and-a-half-hour drive reached Bette's doorstep near midnight. Off and Pennington left immediately and stopped in Englishtown to refuel both the car and themselves. The radio at the diner offered a news flash in the familiar clipped tones of Walter Winchell. Seems that Miss America and her beau, the guru of gossip reported, had eloped to Elkton, Maryland.

They did become something of an item, these two bonded by circumstance and celebrity. Strolling on the boardwalk, they made a photogenic couple—Off dapper in his blazer and slacks, Bette the picture of sweetness rather than sophistication. The pageant committee eventually decreed that Bette could keep her title, and she even warmed to the task a bit, attending parades and participating in radio broadcasts. Her main order of business, however, was to finish high school.

Soon enough, the young couple went their separate ways. The mythology that grew from the curious event reflected the fiction of the lovelorn rather than the unpredictable spin of youthful emotions. One thing is certain. Lou Off was conscripted to be a chauffeur for a Miss America contestant, and he performed his duties to the limit.

War at the Shore

The men wore blue uniforms and carried full packs, as a motorcycle police escort framed their march on Arkansas Avenue from Union Terminal Station to the boardwalk. One hundred strong, they shot no-nonsense glances at the sea, turned (column left), and headed for Virginia Avenue where their quarters awaited at the Hotel Clarendon. At the nearby Elks Club Building, blackboards and radio transmission equipment emerged from trucks at curbside.

The crisp contingent of coast guards marked the onset of a different type of Atlantic City summertime invasion on this late June afternoon in 1942. Thousands more would follow, as would tens of thousands of U.S. Army Air Corps recruits hustled into action during the months after the devastating surprise at Pearl Harbor. Destiny had a payback in store, but at this juncture the Axis forces were peaking, and most American troops needed combat training. The army eyed Atlantic City's skyline of majestic hotels and declared its beachhead.

War Board representatives meeting with hoteliers at the Claridge looked south across a manicured garden to the sweeping terrace of the Marlborough-Blenheim, and beyond to the stocky Dennis and the angular, steepled Shelburne. To the north, the Traymore was a giant camel, a golden multidomed behemoth full of hollows and spires . . . and bedrooms. There were dozens of other hotels and, of course, the glorious expanse of beach. This was a ready-made encampment. The pitch from Uncle Sam was patriotism and "gentle" persuasion. Hitler and the Nazi war machine and the Japanese would have to wait. First, the army would conquer Atlantic City.

Eight A.M. and already Convention Hall was brimming with activity. Moving more swiftly than Manhattan messengers, civilians on roller skates delivered the latest dispatches to ground-floor medical and classification offices. Club-wielding guards fixed the traffic with impassive stares. On the main floor, a sea of undershirts and upraised arms shuffled beneath the massive, arched roof. It was gym class, army style.

Security operatives policed the area, checked the "guard house"

*Limbering up for battle, U.S. Army recruits fill the floor of Convention Hall.
They bunked at Atlantic City's major hotels as the town became a barracks
during World War II.*
PHOTOGRAPH BY FRANK HAVENS, COURTESY COLLECTION OF VICKI GOLD LEVI

where the rest of the crew stood by their bunk beds, then hurried to their second-floor offices to review the day's batch of complaints and requests. Below them, typewriters clacked and files mounted.

The urban acreage of Convention Hall included a four-hundred-car garage, a basement power plant, hundreds of meeting rooms, and a storehouse of equipment. The army had coveted the huge, hangarlike complex as a headquarters and, with bookings reduced and hefty bond payments looming (the structure had been built in 1929 for fifteen million dollars), it was in the city's interest to strike a deal.

Meanwhile, the spacious, fully equipped hotels were ideal barracks. Though the bulky Ambassador had been the first drafted (on June 30), quickly followed by the Traymore with its seven hundred rooms, the Dennis (the last dry spot on the boardwalk), and the Madison, official projections remained guarded. (The army was said to be "establishing a unit" in Atlantic City.) But in rapid succession, the resort's beachfront and side-street hotels signed up for duty—the twenty-nine-story Claridge, formidable Chalfonte–Haddon Hall, swanky Ritz-Carlton, Lafayette, Knickerbocker, Senator, Strand, Brighton, Chelsea, Seaside, President, Breakers, and on—forty-seven in all.

Guests received notices to vacate, then watched workers haul away mirrors and vanities, divans and chiffonniers. Down came the damask draperies and the crystal chandeliers. Dining rooms were transformed into mess halls. Sumptuous suites became crowded bedrooms where soldiers slept on cots and dreamed—often fitfully—of their impending journey across the Atlantic. The queen of seashore resorts became Army Air Force Basic Training Center No. 7.

Some of the hotels were obtained through U.S. District Court condemnation proceedings, most through lease agreements. An *Atlantic City Press* editorial boasted that the town was "cooperating with the government in an hour of crisis." This was no time for the Ice Capades. "The hotel won't be any good if we lose the war," said Claridge General Manager Gerald R. Trimble.

U.S. Senator William H. Smathers and Mayor Thomas Dartnell Taggart Jr. both were courting the army while attempting to inspire the populace and mollify hotel owners. With gasoline rationed, driving restricted, and rail travel curtailed, they argued, Atlantic City could only benefit from guaranteed (though "low-ball") rentals and the spending of a captive crowd. Time would prove that they had genuine foresight. After an early dip, local revenues and real-estate values rose during the war years. For a city still recovering from the Depression, army occupation was the right prescription.

Choice in the matter, though, was largely illusory. The army had come to town and was not about to be displaced. Of course, Atlantic City was born to the role of host, and the citizenry took its cue; shopkeepers, for example, routinely sliced soldiers' bills in half.

While the city retained much of its carefree flavor, BTC No. 7, known locally as "Camp Boardwalk," became the principal Army Air Force training site in the country, a staging area critical to America's eventual success in Europe and the Pacific. Events were moving rapidly for both the world and Atlantic City.

"Atlantic City hasn't seen anything yet," said Major General Walter R. Weaver, as he boarded a transport plane after inspecting the base. "We are fighting the two strongest military nations in the world. They have been preparing for years."

Slanting down a sand dune in the moonlight, the coast guard officer on horseback looked like Lawrence of Arabia. Steadying the animal, he peered into the shadowy distance for possible ships in distress, telltale periscopes, or landed saboteurs.

Yards away, a thin coating of fog had enveloped the boardwalk and shrouded the darkened hotels. At Convention Hall, where spotlights normally shot daggers into the sky, all was in blackness, the fortresslike front not visible to the keenest of eyes. It was a netherworld as unnerving as any London cityscape scouted by Holmes and Watson.

Walking alone on the boards was the headliner of that afternoon's War Bond rally. In her mannish, wide-lapeled jacket and matching, floppy-chic hat, Marlene Dietrich carried her own brand of intrigue. In the thickening mist, she was the only star out.

The great "dim-out" meant shutting off lights cast toward the ocean; placing blue cellophane shields on doors, windows, and lighting fixtures; reducing streetlights to faint rays; and using only parking lights when driving on beach blocks. There had been reports of American tankers and freighters sunk by German U-boats off the southern Jersey coast and, by day, the heroic Civil Air Patrol was providing convoys for the passage of friendly ships and scanning the ocean for enemy subs.

The summer of 1942 was a blur of movement. Everywhere, men were marching in tight formation: in the cavernous Convention Hall, on the boardwalk, at Bader Field, on the northside parade grounds, and the Absecon Boulevard athletic field. They marched in blue or khaki, caps or pith helmets. They marched in "decontamination squads," each soldier sporting high boots, a thick jumpsuit, and a gas mask with a long rubber tube curving to a carrying case of oxygen; past the Warner Theater they marched, as if they had leaped off the screen of a *Buck Rogers* movie.

The memory of chemical warfare in World War I was powerful, and U.S. forces were prepared for such horrors this time. Suitably outfitted trainees were subjected to simulated mustard-gas attacks, first in a tar-papered Quonset hut on Albany Avenue, then in a full-scale mock invasion on the beach during November's Technical Training Command Week, a showcase of army pomp and prowess. A public-address system announced the action, and crowds massed on the board-walk east of Hamid's Pier. When the siege ended, city firefighters doused the pockets of flame remaining on the beach. The production values were worthy of Hollywood.

Other fanfare was less precarious. On Armistice Day (November 11), Air Force recruits marched side by side with vets from the Big War. The AAF's one-hundred-thirty-piece band trumpeted its favorite tune, "Yankee Bugle Call." Soldiers sang with abandon, as visitors supplied fresh lyrics to familiar ditties. Others did jumping jacks in their trousers and sleeveless undershirts in the shadow of beach umbrellas and cabanas. Onlookers crammed the boardwalk railing; behind them, shop awnings flapped in the ocean breeze.

Downbeach on the roof of the President Hotel, above a commodious suite conceived as the "Summer White House," gunners perched next to an automatic artillery piece and searched the skies. On the Brigantine beach, a bivouac featured rows of pitched tents and Red Cross trucks, and at 43rd Street, the rifle range offered beach and ocean targets, pesky mosquitoes, and greenheads bigger than bullets. Recruits assaulted obstacle courses, learned about judo and the nasty uses of the bayonet, and became proficient at the trigger of a submachine gun.

Their steady stream of fire shocked the salt air and, muffled by distance, reached Atlantic City with a popgun staccato that accompanied the clang of the trolleys on Atlantic Avenue and the battle cry of the AAF boys marching in the sunshine: "We're in the air corps now, we're in the air corps now . . . so what the hell are we walking for, we're in the air corps now."

Hundreds of operators sealed off from such clamor tussled with a switchboard of snakes in the New Jersey Bell building on Pacific Avenue, making manual connections in the same room in which air-raid signals were transmitted. The lines were always packed, the operators constantly prepared for emergency calls.

A receiving clerk at the station hospital at Haddon Hall found his job growing busier as casualties began to return from overseas. They weren't all war injuries either. Soon to come were a meningitis outbreak and a measles epidemic.

Sacrifice was an article of faith during the war years. Food and gasoline were rationed, and pleasure driving was penalized by the lifting of gas-coupon books. Hotels converted their heating systems to coal. There were drives to collect scrap rubber, flattened tin cans, and funds for the Red Cross. Meatpacking houses became supply depots. The Fat Salvage Committee of Atlantic City stored bacon grease and assorted drippings for the manufacture of explosives; the National Fireworks plant in Mays Landing was soon producing three thousand tons of bombs per month. Atlantic City had its own War Chest campaign, a War Price and Rationing Board to keep a lid on inflation, and a citizens' liaison committee to handle private complaints. Youth clubs organized special collections, and the American Women's Voluntary Services Organization was all over town—the "Sewing Moms," perhaps the most endearing group of the period.

The Women's Army Auxiliary Corps (WAAC) provided cleaning, laundry, clerical, dental, and pharmaceutical services, and the ranks included occupational therapists and telegraph operators as well as cooks and waiters. Nurses trained for battle conditions, scaling walls and slicing through smoke to reach the "wounded." Atlantic City High School added to its curriculum "pre-induction" courses in radio operations, heating and electricity, and instructions in marching and camouflaging. There were curfews and beach restrictions, blackouts

WAAC-y bunch: The Women's Army Auxiliary Corps was a vital part of the war effort, and even pint-sized ladies—in this case, a very young Vicki Gold—gave soldiers' spirits a huge boost.

PHOTOGRAPH BY AL GOLD, COURTESY COLLECTION OF VICKI GOLD LEVI

and air-raid drills, and this ominous warning from the coast guard: "No enemy aliens allowed on any pier or wharf at any time."

No one, however, was a stranger to the USO. Its various travelers-aid booths and houses provided ready smiles, companionship, card and billiard games, and swingin' dances for thousands of recruits training to be gunners, bombardiers, parachute riggers, propeller experts, mechanics, welders, radio operators, aircraft armorers, weather forecasters, and photographers.

For a while, city and army officials were leery of too warm a reception. The police morals squad was on the lookout for "camp followers" who were "mingling on a too zealously patriotic basis." Mayor Taggart, seeking to enhance his reputation as a crime fighter, vowed to sweep pinballs, pandering, and prostitution from the shore. In his famous "White Line" radio address, he labeled Atlantic City as "overrun with procurers," bemoaned the prospect of military law, and promised an appeal to the state if local forces proved inadequate.

Taggart was fighting a political battle of his own at the time. In May 1942, city commissioners had stripped the mayor of his authority over four departments (including police) by enacting the notorious "ripper" resolution which would later be contested before the state supreme court. Shaping his high profile as a rackets-buster and an influential friend of the army, the bow-tied Taggart jawed and sparred with the commissioners and never stopped trying to regain his full powers. Finally, local law enforcement tightened sufficiently to convince the courts to drop the threat of military rule. The White Line disappeared.

The town became a virtual hospitality center. Under the benevolent command of Colonel Robert P. Glassburn, who resembled then Missouri Senator Harry S Truman, the training base ran smoothly, happily, and on full stomachs. (A typical midday dinner consisted of pork chops, mashed potatoes, bread, and chocolate cake.) Routine took hold: reveille every day at 5 A.M., lights out by 9 P.M. Training stints lasted six weeks or less, depending on individual skill levels. Soldiers marched and sang, and mixed with civilians on the boardwalk. Recreational horseback riders cantered on the beach. The unsavory were stalked by police, and barkeeps were warned to turn away those under the age of twenty-one. Local families served home-cooked meals to lucky soldiers.

Inductees were men, but young men. Homesickness was quite common. The Catholic, Protestant, and Jewish chaplains' offices helped facilitate the granting (and sometimes, extension) of passes, and their staffs made hospital visits. Soldiers received free postcards to send home. Those who needed assistance with writing—due to either injury or illiteracy—found eager volunteers.

The teenage waitress leaned her elbows on the counter and slipped into a daytime reverie as the man in the chef's hat flipped pancakes just behind the front window. Her head was full of Big Band sounds, the crooning of Sinatra, cinema fan magazines, and glossy autographed pictures. But it had room for the ubiquitous, clean-cut GIs drilling and strolling, buying cigarettes and Cokes.

Her daydream ended when the two worlds collided. Into Mammy's, a shake-and-sandwich eatery at the boardwalk end of Central Pier, strode Clark Gable and Ronald Reagan, photoboys supreme. In uniform.

They sat at the counter like two ordinary Joes, and she took their order of coffee and doughnuts. Gable, looking boyish with no moustache, asked for sugar in his brew. Mesmerized, the waiter stared straight ahead and poured a torrent of white granules. Gable sipped, then recoiled as if slapped by Vivien Leigh. Aghast, the waiter checked her condiments: the *salt* shaker was still in the grip of her slender right hand.

Gable smiled, paid the bill (two bits each), and left a dollar tip. Out walked the King and the future Commander-in-Chief.

Backstage at Convention Hall, Kate Smith emerged from a fur coat and hunted for a microphone. As she turned into a narrow passageway behind a curtain, she bumped into the provost sergeant making his rounds. Smith had the facial features of a cherub, but the chassis of a nose tackle. The sergeant was no midget. Their collision was a stand-off.

As Captain Glenn Miller rehearsed his band in the ballroom, a softball tilt was unfolding on the main floor. One of the players—a taciturn fellow from Special Services—glided over the floorboards with a special grace and instinct, and when he stepped to the plate (on the Mississippi Avenue side of the building), workers stopped hammering and the brass came out of second-floor offices to see Yankee Stadium-come-to-Convention Hall. Not one to disappoint, the batter launched a softball on an impossible arc into the balcony on the Georgia Avenue side. Fluid and expressionless, Joe DiMaggio circled the bases.

In 1942, the world was full of both the gallant and the misguided, and the armed forces were no exception. Late that year, Atlantic City resident Arthur Williams became the first New Jersey black to be accepted by the marines. As the army Christmas party displayed a seventy-five-foot tree in Convention Hall, many laid-off hotel employees found work in wartime Washington, where business was brisk.

But not all soldiers felt good will toward all. The army brig on South Carolina Avenue had its share of guests, including seven escapees who hijacked a car and a local minister before being nabbed.

Civilized Atlantic City, though, was prospering. Tax collections, bank balances, and general trade and real-estate revenues were all pointing northward in 1943. The army was paying hotel rentals of only a dollar a day per room, but all rooms were guaranteed every day, and separate fees were paid for the use of dining halls and other space. Moreover, recruits and their visitors consistently reached for their wallets. Consumer confidence was high.

"The army has been the greatest convention Atlantic City ever knew," said Mayor Taggart.

In late May, the army renewed its principal leases, then three weeks later did an about-face and canceled most of the agreements, retaining only Chalfonte–Haddon Hall, the Traymore, and several smaller sites as a hospital complex. The needed training had been completed; the seashore base had served its purpose.

The action shook the city. Hoteliers, now claiming that they had been "pushed around" at the outset, demanded that the government continue rental payments until the following spring. Negotiations grew heated regarding monies due for the use of Convention Hall. (The army finally agreed to pay a retroactive, one-year fee of seventy-five thousand dollars and an equal amount for maintenance and repair.) Atlantic City was a spurned lover.

"[The army] came at the height of the season, and they're leaving us at the same time—but that's war, I guess," said Steel Pier owner Frank P. Gravatt.

But the relationship quickly mended. Bowing to local pressure, a sense of public relations, and a renewed awareness of Atlantic City's appeal to the troops, the army stayed put and simply shifted nameplates. BTC No. 7 officially concluded its business on September 30, 1943. Three weeks later, AAF Redistribution Station No. 1 opened its doors for the reconditioning and reassignment of the "operationally fatigued." Enlisted men bunked primarily at the Ambassador, officers at the Ritz. No reveille, no curfew—just a 12:45 P.M. roll call and unlimited doses of the fabled salt air.

Pilots and gunners strolled about town, or sped by on bicycles. They were grounded, and happy for it. The spotlight now fell, however, on those who returned not fully intact. The station hospital was christened Thomas M. England General Hospital and was for the treatment of patients from all of the armed services. Back they came from Sicily and India and Africa and the jungles of the South Pacific to be ushered from the naval air field in Pomona, or from Union Terminal, by a convoy of trucks and ambulances to the hospital entrance at North Carolina and the boardwalk.

The late Lieutenant Colonel England had slept in the bedclothes of yellow-fever victims in Cuba as the army medical corps sought the origin of that dread disease during the early part of the twentieth century. That kind of resolve was needed at his namesake hospital, dedicated in late April 1944, as soldiers sat in wheelchairs, their lower extremities blanketed against the bracing spring air, backed by an army of Clara Bartons in the huge shadow of Haddon Hall. The speeches were passionate this day, and one army official said it for everyone. "There aren't going to be any apple sellers on any corners after this war."

Connie Mack stood like a lamppost on the boardwalk and surveyed the patients' softball game on the beach. The patriarch of the Philadelphia Athletics didn't spot any Jimmy Foxxes or Mickey Cochranes in the crowd, but he did see a bunch of spirited young men who stopped play and rushed to the railing when they spied his familiar form. At their request, Mack strode onto the sand, shed his coat, and proceeded to umpire the rest of the contest.

Vigor and competition were in evidence elsewhere. On the main floor of Convention Hall, ragged dribblers pounded leather basketballs on three playing courts, including one on the stage. A boxing ring, horse-shoe plots, and multiple courts for shuffleboard, tennis, volleyball, and badminton claimed the balance of the spacious arena.

On the Traymore sun deck, patients moved cautiously on roller skates. Others leaned on crutches or sat in wheelchairs. One man pedaled on a stationary bicycle. His hair was thick and his face unmarked, and his khaki-clad limbs drove forward as if he were whirling around a velodrome. The young man looked whole as well as healthy, but Jimmy Wilson had crashed in a B-25 bomber, and he was a quadruple amputee.

Inside the Traymore, now designated as England General's Convalescent Reconditioning Section, men gritted their teeth and yanked on wooden "shoulder wheels" to revive wounded wings. Amputees removed their prostheses and exercised on specially rigged leg pulleys. Patients played pool and Ping-Pong, swam and danced, learned carpentry and photography. Recovery recognized no limitations.

A hospital aide boarded the jitney on Rhode Island Avenue for a short trip south to North Carolina. He walked under the newly constructed, enclosed wooden bridge connecting the Chalfonte to Haddon Hall, and entered his workplace: the largest hospital in the nation. At its peak, EGH accommodated five thousand patients. On the building's thirteenth floor, private dining rooms had been converted to surgery facilities with a six-hundred-operations-a-month capacity.

England General was a production hub. The artificial-limb shop in the basement of Haddon Hall made a hundred units per month at a cost of up to two hundred dollars each. The pharmacy filled a hundred prescriptions daily. And the hospital's blood-transfusion service was a lifesaver.

Most of the four-thousand-member medical detachment stayed at the Dennis, as did increasing numbers of the infantry returned for rest and reclassification, gladly exchanging their foxholes for downy coverlets. The nurses' quarters were at the Colton Manor, where ivy smothered the lobby façade and trees shaded the entranceway.

Many of the stately hotels were being refurbished by the army and returned to civilian hands. But as the hotels regained their luster and Atlantic City repaired damaged bodies and spirits, and as Allied fortunes brightened overseas, strength ebbed from the nation's great leader.

On April 15, 1945, a lineup of GIs snapped to attention and saluted the flag at half-mast in the courtyard of the Dennis Hotel. Thousands of civilian and AAF personnel jammed Convention Hall for a memorial service. Franklin D. Roosevelt was dead.

By this time, Germany was exhausted, its resources systematically bombed into submission. In May, Victory in Europe (V-E) Day prompted President Truman to caution the obvious: "Our victory is but half won."

The second half required some soul-searching. As the army began to partially demobilize, plans were readied for the discharge of a couple of extraordinary bombs. Following the twin terrors of Hiroshima and Nagasaki, the Japanese surrendered. Stateside celebrations on V-J Day, in August 1945, were a mixture of jubilation and relief. Soldiers danced in the Park Lounge of the Claridge—not a full set of limbs in the house. Smack in the middle of Convention Hall, Private Donald O'Connor tap-danced. In army boots.

A return to normality was welcome in Atlantic City. Bess Myerson, a vision of classic curves and flawless features, was crowned Miss America in September. Throughout the fall, hotel barracks were born again as vacation suites. England General, however, remained at full capacity a while longer.

The army's plans to vacate the hospital sites by March 31, 1946, were met with protests by some two thousand patients anxious to stay at the salubrious seashore. Though the ensuing acrimony (the vets' continued outcry while the army held firm, citing a dwindling patient load) was something of a sour postscript to an otherwise inspiring four-year run, it would be largely forgotten. Emotion yielded to practicality, which is, after all, the army way. The last patient left EGH on June 11.

The hospital complex had treated an estimated hundred and fifty thousand patients in three years. The training and reclassification centers had processed two hundred thousand men. Thousands of nurses and WAACs and merchants and "Sewing Moms" and everyday folk had had a stake in the emotional effort. No other spot on Earth could boast, simultaneously, the madcap antics of Abbott and Costello, the magical trumpet notes of Harry James, the boogie-woogie rhythms of the Andrews Sisters . . . and advanced medical treatment for patients blown out of the sky, blasted from trenches, and released from German and Japanese prison camps.

Then Atlantic City and the entire country shucked the mantle of war and returned to a changed world.

The Hurricane of '44

The party of four at Hackney's restaurant plucked shrimp from a bed of ice and looked through crosshatched windows at the angry sea. One of them, a veteran of World War I, knew all about looming danger and narrow escape. He smoothed his iron-gray hair and returned to his snapper soup. "If there's a problem," he said to his suddenly nervous wife, "we'll be out in plenty of time."

At Atlantic City Hospital, a reclining woman listened to the hypnotic pounding of the rain. She thought of her husband far away on the broad deck of an aircraft carrier and wondered whether he had time to think of her. Then she gasped and patted her swollen stomach; the time was drawing near.

In another hospital—Thomas England General, housed in Haddon Hall—patients blinked at flickering lights and nurses stepped lively down the corridors. This massive army hospital served as a temporary home for thousands of men who had fought overseas and returned less than whole. Now a new enemy was gathering strength in the ocean.

On the boardwalk, rain fell like spears from the sky. Wind-tossed and disoriented, an old woman clung to the railing. The tide raced landward, swallowing the beach and the elaborate sand sculptures that had long dazzled tourists. Schools closed early, sea gulls abandoned their perches, and people brave enough to challenge the gusts wore helmets to deflect flying debris. As Allied troops were penetrating Germany and taking the measure of the Third Reich, the incommensurable forces of nature bore down on the Jersey Shore.

At first it had idled, six hundred and fifty miles off the coast of Miami, a monster in the making. For two days it teased the eastern seaboard and harbored winds up to a hundred and fifty miles per hour. Then, on a Tuesday night in mid-September, it turned northward and moved ominously up the coast. Army and navy fliers dove into the whirlpool to gauge its velocity, and filed their reports. U.S. Weather Bureau officials were calling it the "fiercest in years," and the Hurricane of '44 aimed to live up to its billing.

Florida and the Bahamas were spared serious damage, but when the storm walloped the Carolinas, South Jersey figured to be in its crosshairs. With east-southeast gales reaching hundreds of miles beyond its center, the storm had firepower to match its bad temper. "Strong wind and rain" were expected in Atlantic City on Thursday, September 14. That forecast would prove to be an understatement.

Action began in earnest after noon, and flooding quickly became a problem. Electricity died, public water lines broke, and trains, trolleys, buses, and jitneys ground to a halt. Fish swam into cellars, telephone poles toppled, and schools turned into shelters. Parking-meter heads peeped above the rising water. Bridge tenders shut down their spans. Fire alarms filled the air, but hook-and-ladders were stranded.

One stubborn conveyance, however, moved inexorably forward— a city trash wagon drawn by two thickset horses inched uptown. There, destruction was mounting. A tanker broke free from its moorings and sunk a yacht before foundering. Riptides in the inlet flipped cars, and sand and pilings barricaded the trolley shed near Captain Starn's restaurant. Buildings collapsed, wires dangled dangerously, and sections of the boardwalk scattered in the torrent as if uprooted by a giant hand. Windows shattered at Blatt's Department Store. Heinz Pier yielded sixty feet to the rampaging waters.

In Margate, the boardwalk was a skeleton and the Anglers Club fishing pier was gone except for its clubhouse. Flooded streets mingled boards, chunks of pavement, and roofs of decapitated buildings. The Ventnor Pier, too, was obliterated. Beachfront homes tottered on the brink, and cars squatted motionless on the Atlantic Avenue trolley right-of-way. Boats splintered one another at the marina in Somers Point. Sea Isle City lost its Promenade, Ocean City was under water, and Brigantine was cut off, its bridge to Atlantic City only a memory.

The eye of the storm passed over at five P.M. as residents scrambled for higher ground and city officials sought help. Philadelphia police officers and the U.S. Coast Guard reinforced local police. One other

Among the casualties of the destructive Hurricane of 1944 was Atlantic City's Heinz Pier, severed in two and never to be rebuilt.
PHOTOGRAPH COURTESY COLLECTION OF VICKI GOLD LEVI

group in town joined the battle against the Hurricane of '44: the U.S. Army, which had commandeered the city two years earlier, converting Convention Hall and the grand hotels into a training base by the sea. By September 1944, the camp had been transformed into a "redistribution center" for returning World War II troops, and the military retained its dominant presence in Atlantic City.

When the hurricane hit, soldiers became samaritans. Equipped with muscle, moxie, and specialized vehicles, they snatched many seashore dwellers from the abyss. The old woman floundering on the boardwalk was saved from a watery demise by a soldier who carried her to Convention Hall for treatment along with other orphans of the storm. Soldiers bunking at the Ambassador left that hulking, block-long hotel to rescue a trapped invalid. An army chaplain leaped off a supply truck to aid a woman bear-hugging a tree in Chelsea Park and managed to shepherd her to the President Hotel. Military Police piloted lifeboats and retrieved entire families from swamped cellars.

In one memorable sequence, MPs located thirty-five women and children imprisoned by the inlet floods and guided them to a high-wheeled truck for transport to the Massachusetts Avenue School's makeshift shelter. Amphibious vehicles evacuated the four diners, and seventy-six others, enveloped by the snarling current at Hackney's. Army officers and their wives exited the skinny Ritz-Carlton Hotel for the fortress-like Convention Hall, where an Army Air Force pilot and his bride were taking their vows; fresh from a sprint through the storm, the wedding guests went barefoot.

At Haddon Hall, aides flicked on flashlights and led the way down the winding staircase. Patients wearing pajamas and bathrobes reclined on stretchers; a coast guard brought up the rear. On North Carolina Avenue, high-wheeled ambulances waited to take the evacuees—999 in all—to four trains commandeered for a trip to Halloran General Hospital in Staten Island. The lone patient to remain at England General had broken his back in a fall during an air raid in London. He was a medic.

The delivery room at Atlantic City Hospital was lit by candles and acetylene lights, as two women gave birth and reaffirmed a power of nature more eloquent than any tidal thrashing. The storm got the message and, by nine P.M., departed a wounded South Jersey for points north. People emerged from their huts and shined flashlights into the night, and the sky winked back with a curtain of stars.

Ambulances and trucks clotted the beach block of North Carolina Avenue around noon on Friday, as the army began the ponderous task of emptying England General. The previous day's maelstrom had knocked out the hospital's power plant, and restoring electricity would take time. Along the length of Absecon Island, digging out was the order of the day. Bulldozers pushed mountains of sand toward the boardwalk, and huge pumps lowered water levels on streets and in buildings. Furniture and store goods were piled high on the sidewalk. At Convention Hall, where a generator was coaxing the teletype back to life, army clerks moved their desks and typewriters onto Mississippi Avenue and clacked away in the eighty-five-degree sunshine.

Everywhere, people stared at the upheaval: pianos poleaxed by radiators, walls blasted to rubble as if dynamited, a landscape strewn with wood, glass, cement, and lives in disarray. Three deaths and more than forty injuries were reported in South Jersey. The nationwide death count grew to forty-six, as the hurricane continued its destructive path as far north as New England. Property damage estimates for southern and central New Jersey combined ran between thirty and forty million dollars.

Bricks and mortar, of course, could be replaced. Seeking federal dollars, Governor Walter Edge was already on the phone to Washington. For most, though, the dark day had passed and lives stayed in one piece. Sunbathers returned to the beach as if waking from a bad dream. The sky was a soft blue, a tame sea breeze curled around beach blankets, and the Atlantic Ocean lapped the horizon.

INNOVATIONS & INNOVATORS ✦

The Father of Atlantic City

The doctor stood on a sand dune and gazed at the Atlantic Ocean. Tall and angular with flowing locks framing deep-set, pale eyes and an aquiline nose, he looked as if he had stepped off the pages of a novel. At his side, neighbor Enoch Doughty shared the untrammeled view. Behind them, pine and cedar and bayberry bushes studded an island populated largely by snakes and mosquitoes.

But the expanse of sand and sea before them suggested something else. Something magical. The magic of transformation.

"A city by the sea," said Dr. Jonathan Pitney, adjusting his long cloak ruffled by ocean breezes.

Doughty's vision was more commercial than romantic. "And a railroad to civilization," said the lumberman, a brigadier general in the state militia.

That night, back in the village, Pitney climbed the stairs to the cupola atop the three-story wing he had added to his house two years earlier. From there, he had a panoramic view of inlet and beach. From there, he could reach out and touch the future.

At the exact middle of the nineteenth century, there were just seven residences on Absecon Island, originally dubbed Absegami, or "Little Sea Water," by the Lenape Indians. Cape May already was established as southern New Jersey's tourist destination, and envisioning—much less building—a resort town at Absecon beach required the soul of a sorcerer. As an M.D. and a prominent landowner (five hundred acres'

worth), Jonathan Pitney dealt in the tangible but, above all, craved the challenge of the Big Enterprise. When he would leave his inland rounds to visit a patient on the island, he'd stroll on the sands and take deep draughts of the salt air. Yes, he convinced himself, there were curative powers along this strand—not to mention profit potential.

He had been born in northern New Jersey in Mendham, Morris County, on October 29, 1797, his father, Shubal, a descendant of English immigrants. Jonathan received medical training in New York, but following an apprenticeship at a hospital in Staten Island, the twenty-one-year-old set off for more wide-open spaces. Accounts have him riding on horseback into the village of Absecon in 1819, his saddlebags stuffed with medical supplies. The light was on at Hannah Holmes's tavern, and the first to greet the travel-weary doctor was Enoch Doughty.

The young physician quickly established a busy practice that ranged from English Creek to Port Republic and, occasionally, beyond the marshlands to the beach. He married a local woman (Caroline Fowler) in 1831, and the community felt strongly enough about his professional services to quash his later bid for Congress by organizing a concerted vote for his opponent. Dr. Pitney did not go to Washington.

Clearly, the good doctor was about more than black bags and stethoscopes—Pitney was a political animal. His quick mind and sense of assuredness made him a natural leader and placed him among the powerbrokers. One pleasant evening in 1837, Pitney and Judge Daniel Baker sat on the porch of the judge's Absecon home and talked of splitting Old Gloucester County in two. Soon enough, Old Gloucester's eastern half became Atlantic County, with Pitney as director of the new county's Board of Chosen Freeholders. Seven years later, the ambitious doctor represented his county in Trenton for the framing of New Jersey's new state constitution.

The experience at the state capital would serve Pitney well, for his vision of a spa-by-the-sea included a railroad to transport patrons from Philadelphia, and new railroads needed the lawmakers' blessing. In addition to Doughty, Pitney recruited a cast of persuasive industrialists (mostly glass manufacturers from places like Hammonton and Batsto) to plead his case, and in March 1852, the state legislature chartered the Camden and Atlantic Railroad. Existing railroad barons had a good laugh. Track would never be laid, they figured—how can you build a city on sand and cedar? But Pitney's people saw increased market potential for their glass, pipe, and lumber, and to further capitalize on the enterprise, formed the Camden and Atlantic Land Company (Dr. Pitney a director, of course), which gobbled up acreage on the cheap. The land boom was on.

To preclude a bust, though, someone had to vouch for the project's technical feasibility so that prospective backers from Philadelphia—the planned resort's fountainhead—would invest in the seashore.

That someone was the City of Brotherly Love's own Richard B. Osborne, a civil engineer and early exponent of the mantra "build it and they will come." Osborne, credited with christening the resort "Atlantic City," became Pitney's spiritual partner. While the articulate doctor extolled the benefits of the area's recreational activities and healthful climate, Osborne mapped the railway and pitched investors. The incoming tide foamed dollars and optimism.

Momentum has its prerogatives. On March 3, 1854, the governor approved a municipal charter for Atlantic City. On July 1, the first railroad cars rumbled out of Camden, filled with passengers ferried across the Delaware River from Philadelphia. What they found at the end of the line was not exactly Shangri-la, but for Atlantic City, the ride was just beginning. Dr. Pitney, soon hailed as the Father of Atlantic City, had sired the future Queen of Resorts. In the process, he had increased his personal holdings by some two hundred acres purchased from the Camden and Atlantic Land Company at the bottom of the market.

But Pitney was a man of more than just ideas and an ability to make money. His determined effort to erect a local lighthouse, for example, resulted in scores of saved lives and, in its own way, left a legacy as compelling as the storied city.

Beginning in 1844, in his capacity as notary public (the busy Pitney also had a stint as Absecon's postmaster), he listened with growing compassion to sea captains' tales of wrecked vessels in the waters off Absecon Island. Pitney began petitioning the federal government to fund a lighthouse near the inlet, where treacherous tides often meant death in the darkness. Washington largely ignored him, but when an 1854 northeaster sank the immigrant ship *Powhattan* and some three hundred bodies washed ashore on Absecon beach, Pitney's bid was underscored and thirty-five thousand dollars appropriated by Congress. Lieutenant George Gordon Meade—later of Civil War fame at Gettysburg—engineered construction, and by 1857, "Graveyard Inlet" was flooded with light.

Absecon Lighthouse has retreated from the water's edge and is now a historic shrine. The Dr. Jonathan Pitney House (57 N. Shore Road, Absecon), its original premises built in 1799 and purchased by Pitney in 1824, is a captivating bed and breakfast, its cupola still providing a box seat on the horizon.

As for Atlantic City, the fruition of Pitney's designs and dreams, latter-day master-builders have drawn new maps and altered the skyline. Epochs of wildfire growth, dominance, decline, and renaissance have fixed the city's imprint on American history.

Dr. Pitney, after a lifetime of singing the praises of seashore health and vitality, died at age seventy-two in 1869. Of consumption.

Colonel McKee

Christmas transformed the schoolhouse from a chamber of primers and drab desks to a room full of goodies. Bolts of calico adorned the walls, a glittering tree displaced the lectern, and well-scrubbed children exchanged their multiplication tables for toys, turkey, and candy.

The maker of the feast was John McKee, a veteran of the Civil War and a colonel in the Thirteenth Regiment of the Pennsylvania National Guard. The recipients of his largesse were two dozen farm families who tilled land along a railroad right-of-way in Egg Harbor and Hamilton townships—land leased from the colonel himself. Though his terms were strict, the landlord was widely hailed as a generous man.

That generosity was by design. The colonel had a debt to pay.

Today's McKee City wears different stripes from what its originator intended. Hugging the highway rather than railroad tracks, this Atlantic County acreage is no city at all, but a crossroads of commerce that has replaced tenant farmers with retail shoppers and suburban homeowners. When McKee purchased some four thousand acres of wilderness here beginning in 1884, he fashioned a cooperative farming community tightly reined by rigid leases. That his turf became best known as the home of the Atlantic City Race Course (at the McKee City traffic circle) and, later, as Hamilton Mall, is at odds with his original vision, which saw a safer bet in crop yields. But McKee—a canny, even exploitative, capitalist—surely would have caught the tide of consumerism: the malls, the big brand names, disposable income.

Still, his greatest trademark was himself. It was rare that a black man rose to the rank of colonel in the nineteenth century. Rarer still was a black man of great wealth. John McKee's story is one of distinction . . . and contradictions.

Born in 1821 of slave parents in Alexandria, Virginia, he was set free as a youth and apprenticed to a bricklayer. At age twenty-one, he migrated to Philadelphia and worked in a livery stable, but eventually gained employment at a restaurant, married the boss's daughter, and developed a taste for real estate. With his wife providing the initial capital, McKee acquired a block of row houses and the heady perspective of a landlord.

Come the Civil War, McKee joined Union Negro troops raised in Philadelphia, quickly displayed his leadership qualities, and, it is said, fought valiantly for the North. Afterward, he returned to the Quaker City and a burgeoning career as a realtor. That career, however, may have been built largely on the backs of those emancipated by law but still enslaved by ignorance.

It was a common scenario. Following the Civil War, hordes of former slaves stormed north, unaware of the value of property in the South given them as part of the terms of their freedom. In large northern cities such as Philadelphia, they were fodder for a new breed of master, white or black. Light-skinned and bristling with ambition, John McKee was part of a mulatto population poised to prey on the newcomers.

The deal was simple, if one-sided: offer rental housing in exchange for the abandoned properties down south. Some writers have suggested that McKee, who had accumulated considerable real estate by this time, provided homes for the ex-slaves, while they signed away their land. Adding insult to ignorance, the transplanted tenants still had to pay rent for the privilege.

In this manner, McKee could have acquired his thousands of acres of coal land in West Virginia and holdings in Georgia and Kentucky, some of which he sold, plowing the proceeds into more land in Philadelphia, New York, and New Jersey. At the peak of his prosperity, he was worth two million dollars. Many said that he had a keen eye, but a cold heart; one acquaintance characterized him as "devoid of sentiment."

Yet there was evidence of another John McKee. Philadelphia firefighters remembered his morning greeting punctuated by a two-dollar bill. His eponymous tract in southern New Jersey buttressed order and rationality with a latent yearning for utopia—McKee City sported a sawmill, a frame schoolhouse, a general store, a community hall, stables, sturdy saltbox houses, whitewashed fences, fifty-acre farms in the shadow of the Pennsylvania–Reading Railroad near what is now the Black Horse Pike, and hundred-acre farms along Harding Highway (better known today as Route 40).

Not all his tenants were ex-slaves. One of the hundred-acre farms became the property of Arthur Boerner, a statewide agricultural advocate who served as mayor of Hamilton Township for a time. Boerner came to the area from Philadelphia as a youngster with his immigrant German parents and a sister. His father, Emil, worked on the railroad, and the family at first summered for a couple of years on one of the fifty-acre tracts along the railroad (which parallels West Jersey Avenue). They eventually settled and acquired land along Route 40, where in the late 1990s, the Boerner family was still working the land, generating Pleasant Valley Farm's harvest of apples, blueberries, and Christmas trees.

If Colonel McKee found Santa Claus later in life, his military rigor never abated. Witness the terms of an 1899 lease to one of his McKee City tenants: "A strip 525 feet or two-and-a-half lengths of rope deep, extending the whole width of the farm, is to be cleared by cutting off the wood and brush and burning the same; taking out stumps of trees and hauling them in a pile in back of the house."

The exacting landlord specified the type and quantity of seed to be sown. Cedar trees were deemed untouchable. Tenants who complied for five years could renew for another ten at fifty dollars a year.

The houses that McKee had built were no less attentive to detail, with strong foundations and all walls lathed and plastered. Most of the houses had open front porches and, inside, two rooms on the first floor, three rooms on the second, and two on the third.

This obsessive attention to detail—spiked by a gaudy streak of vanity—framed the intent of what was to be McKee's ultimate legacy, and indirectly caused its undoing.

Compulsion is perhaps most manifest in the desire to control events after one's death. Colonel John McKee died in 1902 at the age of eighty-one. His thirty-six-page will, written two years earlier, provided adequate incomes for his children and grandchildren, but placed the bulk of his estate in trust to the Archdiocese of Philadelphia, with the stipulation that revenues be used to construct a military school for orphans (black and white) in nearby Bucks County.

The Church was taken by surprise—there had been no discussions with McKee, and the colonel was born a Protestant. Emerging tales described a young McKee stricken by smallpox, with only Roman Catholic nuns willing to minister to him. Whatever the religious affiliation, this was to be McKee's postmortem payback.

Hardly an anonymous one, though. McKee's will mandated a bronze statue of the colonel in full uniform, astride a horse, bearing the inscription "Colonel John McKee, Founder of this College." McKee left a photograph for the sculptor and specified that students decorate the pedestal on the Fourth of July and wear brass buttons engraved with the McKee name. The master-builder called for fireproof structures and a complex campus layout. The curriculum was to be based on that of the U.S. Naval Academy.

The school, a sectarian version of Philadelphia's famous Girard College, was never built. McKee had stipulated that his properties remain unsold until the death of his last surviving heir, and twentieth-century inflation had outflanked his estate's revenue stream—that was something the cagey colonel had not anticipated. By the time the final heir died in 1948, the residual estate was insufficient to erect the school as outlined. The matter eventually went to Orphans Court, which preserved the spirit of the bequest by creating a college scholarship fund. Since the 1950s, the McKee Scholarship, administered by the Archbishop of Philadelphia, has granted twenty-five-hundred-dollar annual awards to needy, fatherless boys in the public and parochial school systems.

Meanwhile, in McKee City, where railroad commerce has vanished, farms have dwindled, and the racetrack is in the record books, new shopping plazas sprout near modern, wooded developments, signaling the fragility of legacies, no matter how well planned.

Signs of the Times

At a time when the Atlantic City boardwalk was a profusion of straw hats and parasols, rooftops sprouted billboards that were much more than bearers of information. For people who craned their necks skyward from pavilion benches or rolling chairs, these huge signs delighted the eye as they beckoned the wallet. Their splash of color, bold lettering, and spatial balance captured their maker's art as surely as the advertiser's product. They were part of the architectural landscape.

The maker of that visual feast was the R. C. Maxwell Company, a pioneer in the business and already a presence from the deep South to New England. Maxwell signs told stories (a baker and his bread, a politician and his promises), flirted with pop art (a Ballantine Ale "clock" with hands shaped like bottles), and embraced the public interest (1940s war bonds, draft registration) without discriminating against chauvinists ("Men of New Jersey: Vote No on Women's Suffrage"—1915). They extolled the timeless (Wrigley's Spearmint, Coca-Cola) and the now forgotten (Snowdrift shortening, Red Star yeast). They appeared in ballparks, on clapboard shacks and brick buildings, alongside roadways and railways, . . . and yes, on the boardwalk, where painted images caught the seashore sun, and electric extravaganzas ruled the night.

Uptown, where the foot traffic intensified, Maxwell signs grew larger. A mammoth, rectangular Camel cigarettes billboard fronted the Traymore Hotel, a multidomed structure whose contours paralleled the sign's trademark dromedary. Nearby, a square billboard served up Pabst Blue Ribbon, and on the other side of the Traymore, Miller High Life was on tap. A third brewer, Schmidt's, conveyed its tidings from the top of Mammy's Restaurant at Central Pier. Moving from suds to stogies, Bayuk "Phillies" cigars blended with the beachfront ambience. Maxwell even painted signs for the paint manufacturers: Sherwin Williams covered the earth (actually, a patch of sky) near Haddon Hall, while DuPont touted its "Town and Country" deluxe at the Saratoga Hotel.

*Atop the Million Dollar Pier, the Maxwell Company's Seagram's "horse race" and
Sherwin-Williams sign captured the attention of strollers on the Atlantic City boardwalk.*
PHOTOGRAPH COURTESY COLLECTION OF VICKI GOLD LEVI

If these colorful renderings accented the afternoon, sign-as-
spectacle was reserved for nighttime. Atop Steeplechase Pier, the
double-faced Chesterfield sign (built in 1926) arrayed 26,000 incandes-
cent light bulbs on each side of its 215-foot length and triggered 75-
second cycles of 27-color "steps" climaxed by a heraldic burst of gold
and white bright enough to startle the long dead Lord Chesterfield
himself. On Million Dollar Pier, the animated Seagram's racetrack
sign—relocated from Times Square in 1939—ran four electrified thor-
oughbreds around an oval every three minutes, the changing order of
finish a source of wonder and wagering for onlookers. Just as memorable was the electric diver who appeared to knife right into the ocean
from the Jantzen swimsuit sign. Indeed, Maxwell's penchant for the
dramatic fit the boardwalk's show-biz profile.

Electricity first struck the world of signs in 1891, the year that Robert
Chester Maxwell—still a minor—launched his sign-painting business
in Trenton. His father, Virginia native James Vance Maxwell, had served

with Stonewall Jackson in the Civil War and been appointed "regimental artist" after drawing a caricature of the fearsome general on a latrine wall. (Jackson apparently possessed a sense of humor as well as his celebrated instinct for the jugular.)

Born in the then backwoods town of St. Charles, Missouri, in 1873, Robert Maxwell inherited his father's artistic genes. The wooden sides of any barn in the South were potential canvases for his imagination and paintbrush. Orphaned at age nine, he surfaced eight years later in Trenton, where he established the firm incorporated in 1894 as the R. C. Maxwell Company.

The young Maxwell had a feel for the marketplace. Rail travel predominated in the late nineteenth and early twentieth centuries, and the Maxwell Company's custom-designed, elongated billboards hugged the tracks, enabling passengers to read the entire message as the train whizzed past. When America fell in love with the automobile, Maxwell signs—frequently bordered by shrubs and encased in homey, latticed frames—greeted motorists on newly paved highways. Coca-Cola was an early customer, and soon the red-lettered script became as familiar as a sunrise. (The apotheosis of the Maxwell "Coke" signs was an electric dazzler that "bubbled" in New York's Columbus Circle.) Advertisers ranged from Pillsbury to appliances, sugar to shingles, campgrounds to ground beef, widgets to Westinghouse.

Several Coca-Cola signs joined the boardwalk lineup in Atlantic City, where Maxwell had built an "electrical shop" on New York Avenue in the mid-1920s. In this modest, two-story structure, designers and technicians conceived the company's electrified, marquee attractions. Less elaborate creations emerged from the billboard shop next door, where a camera perched on a tripod was cloaked by a black drape, and colors were hand mixed for clients. The color "spice rack" had its reds (Tuscan, Venetian, vermilion), blues (Prussian, cobalt, oasis), and a spectrum of other colors, many not seen beyond the Maxwell universe.

Those who applied these colors to wooden planks, brick façades, and paneled posterboard shared a streak of courage and a well-honed sense of proportion. The "wall dogs" often braved precarious scaffolds to decorate the heights, and fitting a sign's layout within a prescribed space was clearly a task for an artisan-cum-architect. This skilled work itself was captured on a canvas (now residing in the company's archives) by one "Mac" McGoldrick, a practitioner of the outdoor art for fifty years at Maxwell. His painting of the corporate "mascot" shows a man plying his trade while seated on a narrow, suspended platform, additional brushes and cans of paint at the ready. It seems yanked right out of the Norman Rockwell portfolio.

"He [McGoldrick] would paint a sign and never have to look at it," says David Maxwell, who has piloted his father's company into the next century.

The great Chesterfield sign collapsed in a hail of sparks when fire ravaged the Steeplechase Pier in 1932. The same fate befell the Seagram's sign in 1949, and the electric horsemen rode no more. The intrepid wall dogs retired and entered the Pound of Fame. Their trade, like much of civilization, has grown increasingly high-tech.

But plain, old, oversize billboards—static, but rarely dull—refuse to go out of style. In the late 1990s, the R. C. Maxwell Company, still headquartered in Trenton, maintained its seashore tradition. Many of the existing billboards on the Atlantic City Expressway, the White Horse and Black Horse pikes, and Atlantic and Pacific avenues were Maxwell-made. The company did business with all of the casino-hotels and was the largest outdoor sign maker in Atlantic County. Maxwell billboards also remained prominent in Mercer, Burlington, and Cape May counties, and in Ocean County south of Barnegat.

Structural changes have simplified the modern billboard. Many of the standard, fourteen-by-forty-eight-foot displays are now supported by a single steel pole rather than the old paradigm: several upright poles anchored by slanted wooden braces sunk in the ground. In addition, vinyl graphics sometimes replace paint, and sign panels are often prefabricated and assembled on-site.

But though modernized, this solid, conventional craftsmanship is quite apart from the computer-age wizardry apparent in such electronic displays as the Caesar's and Trump Plaza signs facing the Atlantic City "Gateway" at Atlantic and Missouri avenues. Such signs change copy by computer, and costs run high. Rather than cyberspace signs, some Maxwell veterans anticipated a comeback of neon.

Though flickering neon lights evoke back alleys and film noir hotels, the neon they had in mind is a warm flood of color; whether it's Vegas garish or vintage glitter is all in the mix. The R. C. Maxwell Company, you see, was a master-mixer.

By wattage or brushwork, the finished product always sparkled.

Sara Spencer Washington

The woman's patience was wearing thin. The salesclerk, young and officious, had asked her—no, told her—to wait, and she had done just that, as the clerk kept busy with a succession of fresh customers. The woman wore a silk-brocaded dress beneath her wool coat and a serious expression behind her glasses, but the only thing the clerk had noticed was the color of her skin: darker than most of the furs on display for well-heeled Christmas shoppers on a mid-December afternoon.

And so the woman waited. For a while.

"Excuse me."

The salesclerk looked up from her order slip, her forehead too furrowed for her twenty-odd years. Behind her, a blue-haired dowager was ogling a sea of sable.

"I'm sorry; I'll be with you as soon as I can." Her tone of voice belied her—she wasn't particularly sorry.

What happened next could not have been scripted any better by a team of Warner Brothers script writers. The department supervisor, who had begun her career at Wanamaker's twenty years earlier during Philadelphia's Sesquicentennial, sauntered by and saw the lady-in-waiting.

"Mrs. Washington," the supervisor said warmly. "Back again?"

Sara Spencer Washington returned the supervisor's smile.

"I'd like to get one more."

The supervisor quickly sized up the situation and flashed a mirthless smile at the salesclerk.

"Another mink, my dear"—and drawing closer, in an icy whisper—"now."

Madame Sara Spencer Washington demonstrated the power of initiative, building an international business and a reputation for self-reliance.
PHOTOGRAPH COURTESY COLLECTION OF VICKI GOLD LEVI

The year was 1946, and while Sara Spencer Washington could write two forty-six-hundred-dollar checks to the same department store on the same day without breathing hard, the nickel-and-dime prejudice of the wider world still consigned her to second-class status. But Madame Washington, as she came to be known, was a devastating counter-puncher. When a certain restaurant refused to serve her, she decided to rent the joint for the evening; she sued another balky eatery right down to the linens. The same year that the Wanamaker salesgirl slipped up, ssw launched Atlantic City's flip-side Easter Parade on Arctic Avenue, and black women in furs and broad-brimmed hats graced the rotogravure in a show of force and finery.

Who was this woman of means and moxie? She had been honored at the 1939 World's Fair in New York as one of the planet's "ten most distinguished businesswomen." Cosmetics was her business, but her impact was far more than skin-deep.

Born Sara Spencer in Virginia in 1889, she came north in 1911, serving notice right away that entrepreneurship was not the province solely of white males. After sampling the business climate in Philadelphia, she shifted to Atlantic City, establishing a one-room beauty shop on the first floor of an Arctic Avenue building she would eventually own.

Ssw saw well beyond those four walls and had the drive to pursue her vision. Hairdressing was a respectable trade, but there were only so many manes one could massage. Larger opportunities awaited those who recognized them—and seized them.

And so, ssw turned teacher, grooming the next generation of beauticians; and purveyor, canvassing neighborhoods with existing and self-styled products. Inevitably, expansion followed. She received a patent for a hair curl-removal system. "Glossatina" ensured sheen, pomades celebrated slick. Hot-comb pressing oils soothed the scalp. Perfumes, lipstick, and facial creams joined the lineup.

Ssw went corporate. Her Apex Schools of Scientific Beauty Culture boasted four thousand graduates a year and set up shop in a dozen American cities, South Africa, and the Caribbean. Four other companies sprouted under the Apex banner, as the business encompassed drugstores and publishing (a national beauty magazine) as well as hair salons. Boxcars of raw materials poured into a laboratory on Indiana Avenue in Atlantic City and seventy-five different Apex products emerged, to be ushered by a fleet of trucks to forty-five thousand Apex agents. Ssw knew all about vertical integration.

She presided over her empire from her home office at Indiana and Arctic and also hosted social functions at that stately, four-story structure. Her well-tended appearance was a billboard for her company, and her bearing commanded respect, though a warm smile in several photographs suggests accessibility.

Indeed, Mme. Washington funneled some of her wealth into the community and has been characterized as a "latent activist." Her Apex Rest offered furnished rooms and recreational facilities at a time when African Americans had to search hard for either. Apex Hall routinely converted its dance floor into a basketball court, so colorful maestro Cab

Calloway could yield to future New York Knick "Sweetwater" Clifton. The Apex Country Club, a nine-hole course carved out of the woods of Pomona in the late 1940s, put blacks on the links long before Tiger Woods; now Pomona Golf Course, Apex C. C. offered sandy fairways, well-kept greens, and a place where racial boundaries didn't apply.

Mme. Washington extended her persona to the political arena, serving as an Atlantic County Republican committee representative in 1938, and backing future state banking commissioner Horace Bryant in his successful run for Atlantic City commissioner. In the 1940s, she formed an alliance of sorts with flamboyant evangelist "Father Divine"—his acolytes bought her products; she purchased his Brigantine Hotel, precipitating the first integrated beachfront in Atlantic City.

Her second husband (she had parted with Isaac Washington at the end of World War I), Shumpert Logan, became active in her business, but she was still Madame Washington to the business world and the social order of the day. She could be photographed with the Astors and Huttons, but Atlantic City's north side remained home base to the end.

"She was held in awe by young folk," said Sid Trusty, who recalled a few visits to the erstwhile landmark at Indiana and Baltic, and whose storehouse of local African-American memorabilia is rather awe-inspiring itself.

Stamina was ssw's long suit. After a stroke paralyzed her in 1947, she battled back to regain her voice and, ultimately, dispensed with the cane; she never did need much assistance. When death finally claimed her in March 1953, she left an estate of more than one million dollars—a considerable sum in those less inflated times. Adopted daughter Joan Cross Washington (now Hayes) assumed the presidency of Apex, but time was short for the symbolically named company. By the early 1960s, the business was absorbed by a Baltimore firm. The last line of Apex products spotted in the marketplace was produced in Memphis, the name surviving if not the company.

The name Sara Spencer Washington survived and received a new gloss, courtesy of the Atlantic County Women's Hall of Fame. At the Hall's annual banquet in 1997, the round of inductees included Mme. Washington, the "first female in the county to own a national manufacturing corporation."

Grandchildren Saverne and Wesley Hayes were on hand to celebrate the occasion. Their grandmother had been a canny promoter and a woman bent on financial independence . . . but much more. She had tasted power yet remained sober, understood glamour but prized integrity above all, stressed the importance of economic progress for black people—and all people.

And endured salesclerks with attitudes.

Seabrook Farms

Charles F. Seabrook, better known as C. F., stepped up to the scale. This was no ordinary weigh-in. It was June 1950 in Upper Deerfield Township, Cumberland County, and the sixty-nine-year-old chairman of Seabrook Farms was out to prove a point.

To demonstrate the economic impact of Seabrook Farms on surrounding South Jersey communities, Seabrook had organized a "Cavalcade of Cartwheels," cartwheels being a slang term for silver dollars. For two weeks, the man described as the "Henry Ford of Agriculture" by *Forbes* magazine for applying industrial and assembly-line techniques to farming would pay the company's more than three thousand employees in silver dollars. The cash registers of area merchants would be weighted down with a surge of Seabrook silver.

The event was a public relations dream. More than two-hundred-fifty-thousand silver dollars were transported by armored car from the Federal Reserve Bank in Philadelphia to Seabrook, just north of Bridgeton, and state troopers were brought in to provide security. And Seabrook had agreed to donate to charity a sum of money equal to his weight in silver dollars—$2,560 in cartwheels for his 160 pounds.

The impact of Seabrook Farms went beyond the borders of South Jersey. On fifty thousand acres, Seabrook Farms produced 15 percent of the country's frozen vegetables, making it the world's largest farming-freezing operation. Called the "biggest vegetable factory on earth" in a January 1955 *Life* magazine article, Seabrook Farms produced enough asparagus in 1954 to feed one serving to every resident of New York, Florida, Washington, and Texas.

All of this was accomplished with a workforce that resembled a miniature United Nations. In the years during and after World War II,

Workers check out the peas at Seabrook Farms. The peas were kept in hoppers and were washed, blanched, sorted, and finally packed into retail and institutional packages.

PHOTOGRAPH COURTESY OF SEABROOK EDUCATIONAL AND CULTURAL CENTER

Seabrook Farms employed people from more than thirty countries on four continents—most of them war refugees and Japanese Americans held at the start of the war. The agricultural field at Seabrook resembled a global village where at least two dozen languages were spoken.

The guiding force behind the operation was C. F. Seabrook, whose father, Arthur, launched the family's agricultural empire when he began farming on sixty-three acres of land in Deerfield Township in 1893. C. F. displayed an early aptitude for farming when at the age of fourteen he began experimenting with overhead irrigation. He found he was able to increase the production of celery by up to 300 percent, and, by 1912, the younger Seabrook had taken over management of the farm from his father.

C. F. introduced industrial techniques such as assembly lines and research into the business of agriculture. He set up an engineering company to build roads, railroads, buildings, and cold storage facilities for his growing agricultural empire. The outbreak of World War I, in 1914, created a demand for food and caused prices for agricultural products to skyrocket. By 1921, Seabrook Farms had expanded to four thousand acres with three hundred acres under irrigation. Six greenhouses covered ten acres, and the workforce had grown to include five hundred employees who lived in housing built by the company.

The expansion may have been a case of too much too fast. Seabrook was forced to relinquish control of his farm in 1924. Improved transportation allowed crops from the southern states to be sold in New Jersey markets before Seabrook's crops could be harvested. Two New York investors—W. A. and A. M. White—who supplied the money for expansion took control of Seabrook Farms and renamed in Del Bay Farms, Inc.

Del Bay Farms would have its own financial problems. Seabrook rounded up new investors and bought back his company in October 1929, just before the stock market crashed. It was a struggle for farmers all over during the Great Depression, but Seabrook, with the help of his sons Belford, Courtney, and Jack, devised ways to keep the farms afloat. Faced with a surplus of cabbage, Belford Seabrook, C. F.'s oldest son, supervised the building of a plant for producing and canning sauerkraut. Similar efforts were made with Seabrook-raised cattle, carrots, and potatoes; ingredients for beef stew that were distributed to families on relief by New Jersey officials.

The elder Seabrook gave his sons responsibility, even at young ages. At fourteen, Belford was a foreman on the construction of Route 77, while Jack at thirteen served as a vegetable grader.

In the 1930s came the quick freezing of vegetables, a technique of preserving produce that guaranteed a longer shelf life for the company's products. In some cases, less than an hour would elapse from the time a vegetable was picked and washed until it was frozen in the company's twenty-three-acre processing plant. The end product would be packages of Seabrook products shipped to stores in states east of the Mississippi River. In its peak years after World War II, Seabrook Farms would grow nearly two dozen types of vegetables (from asparagus to wax beans) and fruits (from boysenberries to strawberries).

The Japanese attack on Pearl Harbor on December 7, 1941, created a strong demand for Seabrook Farms products to feed the nation's armed forces. At the same time, the military draft depleted the manpower needed to run the company's farms. Seabrook's solution was the recruitment of people displaced by the war. About twenty-five

Trucks carrying vegetables and fruits grown at Seabrook Farms were a common sight on the nation's highways during the 1950s and 1960s. This was an early version of the refrigerated tractor-trailers used for frozen-food delivery. The compressors were powered by a dual-voltage motor, 24 volts while on the road and 110 volts when parked at a warehouse.
PHOTOGRAPH COURTESY OF SEABROOK EDUCATIONAL AND CULTURAL CENTER

hundred Japanese Americans from the West Coast, who had been placed in internment camps after the war broke out, came to work at Seabrook Farms beginning in 1944.

"Most of the people who came here to work had nothing; they were starting their lives all over again," said John N. Fuyuume, executive director of the Seabrook Educational and Cultural Center, a museum, in the basement of the Upper Deerfield Township municipal building, dedicated to the Seabrook legacy. Fuyuume came to Seabrook to work as a teenager while he was off from college. His Japanese-American parents preceded him, and he opted to remain in South Jersey after the war ended.

Other workers came from outside the United States, including prisoners of war from Germany and refugees from Austria, Russia, Italy, and the Baltic states of Estonia, Latvia, and Lithuania.

The company was able to overcome the multiple language barrier. Seabrook management chose bilingual supervisors to ensure work was not interrupted. Seabrook Farms also published company newspapers in a variety of languages, including English, Spanish, Japanese, and Estonian, to keep the workers informed.

The decade after World War II was a time of peak production for Seabrook Farms. With crops growing on fifty thousand acres in

Cumberland, Salem, Cape May, Atlantic, Gloucester, and Burlington counties, Seabrook produced about ninety million pounds of fruits and vegetables annually. Seabrook owned about half the land and contracted with local farmers on the other half—a total area almost forty-two times the size of Atlantic City.

However, C. F. Seabrook's health problems cast a cloud on the company's future. The family patriarch had suffered a stroke in the fall of 1941 at the age of sixty. Health problems would continue on and off in the 1940s and 1950s. Relationships between Seabrook and his sons became strained. In May 1959, Seabrook bypassed his sons and sold his controlling interest in the company to Seeman Brothers. Seabrook's sons sold their stake in the company, ending an era in South Jersey agricultural history.

Seeman Brothers never achieved the level of success of its predecessor. The company's fortunes declined in the 1970s and the workforce had dropped to under a hundred employees when the company shut its doors in March 1982.

The Seabrook family was not out of the farming business for good, though.

Seabrook Brothers and Sons began operating in 1977 under the direction of James M. Seabrook and Charles F. Seabrook II and their children. The company was able to buy back the name of Seabrook Farms in 1994. The company's old slogan—"We grow our own, so we know it's good, and we freeze it right on the spot"—was applicable once again as the next generation of Seabrooks carried on the family's agricultural legacy into the twenty-first century.

Seashore Architect: Vivian Smith

The young draftsman walked to his office window and looked down at the Philadelphia streets, where dray horses pulled wagons and trucks loaded with milk, ice, or scrap metal. His eyes rose gradually to the rooflines of broad-shouldered buildings that housed the city's commerce: hotels, a department store, a newspaper headquarters, structures of stature and solid design. It was a new century, and emerging cityscapes captured the architectural eye. To make an imprint, though, one first needed imagination.

Still in his teens, Vivian B. Smith had both imagination and the ambition to convert it to reality. He envisioned commodious, inviting hotels, office buildings that used space wisely yet retained a certain grace, meeting halls of dimension and decorative flair. And he planned to make his vision tangible not in Philadelphia or New York—the two urban Goliaths of the Northeast—but on the sand and soil of his native southern New Jersey.

If buildings are symbols as well as shelter, then City Hall—that crucible of local government—should reflect the tenor of the community. At the dawn of World War I, seashore towns were coming of age, and more than eight decades later, the sweep and power of Ocean City's city hall still express its civic ambition. The front steps climb steeply to formidable columns and an arched vestibule that draws visitors into the shadows. There is a romance with detail: pediments cap casement windows, pedestals bear iron lighting fixtures, terrazzo floors sport tile borders, wood pilasters bedeck interior walls.

Vivian Smith designed his hometown's city hall in 1914, invoking the beaux-arts classical style, which synthesized familiar Greek and Roman forms. He had been born in Ocean City in 1886 and attended Ocean City High School before seeking out the wisdom of big-city architects in Philadelphia. Now he was back at the shore and full of creative energy. The 1920s brought a series of commissions that altered both neighborhoods and skylines. In Ocean City, Smith unveiled the stately Flanders Hotel and the new Music Pier and transformed his modest high school alma mater into a citadel of learning.

In Ventnor, he designed a homey city hall, a glorious community church, and numerous schools and residences of distinction; in Atlantic City, the Breakers Hotel and several apartment and commercial buildings that made an architectural statement, but never at the expense of their surroundings. He fashioned schools and department stores, shops and plants, the lofty and the compact. And long before all of this, he built a city.

During the World War I years, Smith designed and oversaw the construction of the Bethlehem Steel Company town of "Belcoville," one of several U.S. production hubs aiding the war effort. Situated a few miles south of Mays Landing, Belcoville was home to five thousand

The stately, imposing Flanders Hotel in Ocean City is perhaps the hallmark of architect Vivian Smith's career.
PHOTOGRAPH BY ELIZABETH WILK

people, and its blueprint called for churches, stores, a theater, and a town hall to join the huge munitions plant. Showing a talent for organization and creativity, Smith supervised an industrial army that laid the infrastructure and erected the buildings. Other wars have since come and gone, and today's Belcoville, next to county parkland, is more bucolic than martial.

By the late 1920s, Smith's reputation as the consummate seashore architect was secure. His Atlantic City offices at the Guarantee Trust Building rubbed elbows with some of his most distinctive works: the Segal Fruit Building with its copper canopy and garlanded doorways, the main auditorium of Chelsea Baptist Church on Atlantic Avenue, the French Gothic-flavored Elks Club building with its mansard roof and porte-cochere off Virginia Avenue, the Senator Hotel complete with cupola and sky cabana overlooking the beach block of South Carolina Avenue, and the regal Breakers on New Jersey, its rooftop garden and majestic entrance facing the Garden Pier.

In Ventnor, where Smith lived on Dudley Avenue with his second wife, Josephine, and their two children, his sense of fit and proportion was embodied by the Community Church, which still beckons worshipers at Victoria and Ventnor avenues. The stone pile climbs to a bell tower and features a massive stained-glass window, but its overall configuration blends into the residential neighborhood. The architect had the same objective in mind when he designed Ventnor City Hall, built in 1928 and still the fulcrum of the community. Like its Ocean City counterpart, it marries brick and terra-cotta outside, wood and marble inside. But Smith wanted the Ventnor building to be more pub than palace.

"The idea was to put a municipal building in a residential setting," said Penny Watson, whose Bridgeton firm of Watson & Henry Associates was the consulting architect for the 1990s restoration projects at both the Ventnor and Ocean City city halls.

Watson pegged the Ventnor building's architectural style as "Jacobethan" (a combination of Jacobean and Elizabethan), and said that the look is that of an English "moot hall," the atmospheric venue where the early Brits gathered to flex their political and judicial muscles. From the sweeping elegance of the Breakers to the timbered warmth of Ventnor City Hall, Vivian Smith demonstrated versatility and an awareness of architecture's psychological impact.

Ocean City's Music Pier opened amid bunting and blaring horns on July 4, 1929, and the music hasn't stopped since. Vivian Smith sought a structure of seaside grace as well as acoustical fidelity, and equipped it with a furnished solarium and an adjacent loggia swept by ocean breezes. It is the perfect spot for a Puccini aria or a Gilbert and Sullivan showstopper to boom through the night and wrap around a moonlit deck.

A few blocks down the beach, the Flanders Hotel, renovated in recent years, once again welcomes guests. This genteel building always seemed the epitome of a seashore hotel, and its red terra-cotta roof has long been the signature of the Ocean City skyline. Elsewhere in Smith's Ocean City, work crews have chased a century's wear and tear from the Ninth Street wall of City Hall. And the high school, a castle of brown brick and notched rooflines, still turns out a fresh batch of grads each spring.

Indeed, Smith's work continues to resist the encroachment of time and modernization. Handsome residences retain their vintage vigor in

Northfield, Ventnor, and Chelsea. Of the two Ventnor elementary schools that Smith designed, one remains: The former Troy Avenue School is now part of Ventnor Professional Campus, a center for small business. In Atlantic City, where in later years Smith moved his practice to the prestigious Real Estate and Law Building on Atlantic Avenue, the Chelsea Baptist Church still gives pause with its swirl of turrets and battlements, and its prominent sign "Christ Died for Our Sins."

Of course, even the most powerful vision is not eternal, and buildings are as mortal as their creators. During recent decades, some two dozen local buildings designed by Vivian Smith have met the wrecking ball. The Breakers fell in 1974, the ornate Elks Club building long before that. Also vanished are Hotel Donato (near Atlantic City's present City Hall), the tidy Crailsheim Apartments on Illinois Avenue (now a Sands Casino-Hotel parking lot), and many other stores, apartments, and office buildings noteworthy for their clean lines, Gothic tracery, and functional comfort.

One that remains provides a window on the past. On the southeast corner of North Carolina and Atlantic avenues, the former Segal Fruit Building (renamed the Commerce Building) now houses purveyors of less juicy commodities. Girdling the beige-brick walls, the copper canopy has been oxidized aquamarine. Partially visible behind its faded façade is the building's original name and the designation "Fancy Fruits." Even those with perfect vision must squint to make it out.

By the time Vivian Smith died in 1952, his architectural style had receded into history. The contemporary look was becoming sleeker, simpler, less fancy. Symbolism was now left to poets and painters.

Smith belonged to another time. He saw a wide-open seashore and gave it a classical identity. And much of his work became classic.

The Blue Comet

Like a first kiss, we never forget our first set of trains. For my father, it was the Blue Comet, a model train made by the Lionel Corporation. He received the trains, a toy he would keep for the rest of his life, as a Christmas present at the age of eight in 1930.

In one sense, to call the Blue Comet a toy is misleading. It is more a work of art than a plaything. When hooked together, the engine, coal car, and three passenger cars measure seventy-eight inches in length. It traveled around a nine-foot oval track. Its retail price—seventy-five dollars—was as impressive as its size during the Great Depression.

The craft and attention to detail that went into the train would make a child—and more importantly, a parent—forget the cost. Painted a sleek blue, the passenger cars seem to gleam in the light. The car's removable roof reveals the train's interior—individual seats less than an inch wide to accommodate the miniature passengers. No detail is considered insignificant. The restroom contains a miniature sink and a toilet with a seat that goes up and down.

For my father, trains had the ability to transcend childhood. Except for his years in the army during World War II and until his death in 1989, the train was set up each year during the Christmas season, a yuletide fixture in our household as much as the Nativity scene and the Christmas tree. During the 1960s, my father turned down offers of five thousand dollars from train collectors to sell his treasured Blue Comet.

In real life, the Blue Comet was no less impressive. Billed as "The Seashore's Finest Train" by the Central Railroad of New Jersey, it ran from New York City to Main Station at Arkansas and Arctic avenues in Atlantic City from February 1929 to September 1941. The idea behind the creation of the train was simple: to compete with the Pennsylvania Railroad for the lucrative passenger business between New York and Atlantic City.

The railroad had designed the Blue Comet as a deluxe coach to replace its mixed coach and parlor car service. The Blue Comet offered first-class service to coach passengers at regular fares. Designers made it visually appealing to passengers and passersby, making it an effective public relations tool as the cars streaked along the tracks like a comet crossing the skies. This was no mere mechanical train but a form of transportation that exuded personality, character, and flair.

From the locomotive to the observation platform, the exterior of the train was finished in Packard blue, Jersey cream, and royal blue. A cream-colored stripe ran the length of both sides of the train to suggest the surf, sky, and sandy beach along the Jersey Shore. The interior was furnished and decorated in tones of blue from the porters' uniforms to the table service and linen.

The color scheme even extended to the tickets, printed on blue paper. Each ticket carried a number and letter to designate the coach and seat the passenger had been assigned. It was similar to getting a reserved-seat ticket for a sporting event. No seats were sold for the observation and smoking cars to allow all passengers full access to all facilities on the Blue Comet.

At the top of the three locomotives used on the line, the words "The Blue Comet," printed in gold, identified the train. Each of the sixteen cars was named for a comet. The dining car, for example, was named Giacobini, while other cars bore such names as Halley, Westphal, and Holmes.

Service on the Blue Comet kicked off on February 21, 1929, and symbolized the notion that anything was possible during the era of prosperity known as the Roaring Twenties. Advance word and publicity about the train had piqued the public's interest.

Hundreds had turned out to see the train at Red Bank, Monmouth County, on its February 17 trial run. Although the train was publicized as running from New York to Atlantic City, the first leg of the trip was by boat. Passengers from Manhattan had to take a fifteen-minute ferry ride to Jersey City where they boarded the Blue Comet.

The train traveled from Jersey City to Atlantic City, a distance of 136 miles, in three hours, stopping along the way in Newark, Elizabeth, Red Bank, Lakewood, and Winslow Junction before reaching its final destination. Two round-trips were run daily during the train's early years of service. Departure times from New York were at 11 A.M. and 3:30 P.M.; the train left Atlantic City at 9:15 A.M. and 4:15 P.M. Additional trips were added on weekends during the summer months. The cost of a round-trip ticket was $8.40.

Initially, the Blue Comet was a roaring success. With speeds reaching between eighty and ninety miles an hour, it reached its destination on time an eye-popping 97 percent of the time during its first five years. Standards for measuring this were more stringent back then, since the train had to be in the station, not just within sight of it, to be considered on time. During its first year of operation, it carried 62,105 passengers.

One of the selling points of the train was its dining car, which could accommodate thirty-six people at one seating. A full-course dinner, featuring main courses such as baked fresh sea trout or roast beef cost only $1.25, while the Blue Comet Special Plate Dinner was a culinary bargain at 75¢. A favorite among diners was the heated apple pie topped with a slice of New York cheddar cheese.

The residents who lived along the Blue Comet's route developed a special relationship with it. Often, hundreds of people would assemble

The Blue Comet attracts a crowd at Red Bank on February 17, 1929.
PHOTOGRAPH COURTESY OF TOM WILK

along the tracks to catch a glimpse of the train streaking by. Crew members would toss daily newspapers off the train to people who lived in remote areas of the Pine Barrens, through which the Blue Comet traveled. To return the favor, local residents would deliver to the Lakewood stop buckets of wild blueberries or raspberries they had picked from the woods.

New Jersey Central realized it had something special with the Blue Comet. Birthday parties for the train were held in February of each year. In 1934, the fifth birthday party included the installation of five electrical candles on the locomotive. The Blue Comet got a promotional boost in its early years. A Lionel Corporation executive who often rode the train persuaded the company to produce a model set of the trains in 1930.

Despite its goodwill with passengers, events beyond the Blue Comet's control eventually would put the train out of business. Chief among them was the stock market crash of October 29, 1929, only eight months after the inception of the Blue Comet's service. With the nation's unemployment rate at 25 percent by 1932, train rides were a luxury few people could afford. Ridership on the Blue Comet fell from

02,105 in 1929 to 17,351 in 1933. Revenue generated by the train fell from $303,043 in 1930 to $66,901 in 1940. In 1939 and 1940 combined, the Blue Comet lost more than $108,000.

But the Central Railroad of New Jersey and the Blue Comet did not go down without a fight. The railroad reduced fares for the Blue Comet in 1936, resulting in a temporary increase in riders. However, it was a short-term recovery, as the number of riders fell to 13,668 in 1939, the lowest in its history. In an effort to cut its losses, the railroad owners filed a petition for bankruptcy in October 1939. The railroad had unpaid taxes of $7.2 million for 1932 and 1933.

Ready to throw in the towel, the railroad filed an application with the Public Utilities Commission in March 1940 to discontinue the Blue Comet service. Atlantic City Mayor Charles D. White appealed to the panel to keep the train in service, saying the resort would suffer if service were stopped.

The Blue Comet would get a reprieve for an additional eighteen months, but the commission allowed the railroad to pull the plug effective September 28, 1941, ten weeks before the United States entered World War II.

In the aftermath of the war, transportation habits would be revamped. Americans' love affair with the automobile would silence the iron horse as luxury trains would go the way of silent movies. The Blue Comet has been gone for more than half a century, but two of its passenger cars, stripped of their seats and other interior fixtures, rest on a rail off the White Horse Pike in Winslow Junction. The cars offer a silent tribute to a shining moment in New Jersey railroad history.

Teflon Changes the World

When it comes to food and food preparation, the name of Dr. Roy J. Plunkett has largely been overlooked. However, Plunkett's achievement—the discovery of Teflon—can stand alongside such culinary innovators and innovations as Julia Child and The Food Network.

Plunkett's discovery of the technology that made nonstick kitchenware possible forever changed the way food is prepared and cooked. But Teflon, known as the world's most slippery solid, nearly slipped through the hands of the South Jersey scientist.

Plunkett's moment in the scientific spotlight occurred at Jackson Laboratory, a part of DuPont's Chambers Works in Deepwater, Salem County, on April 6, 1938.

The day began uneventfully as the twenty-seven-year-old Plunkett and Jack Relak, his lab assistant, were working on a new refrigerant as part of a study of fluorinated hydrocarbons.

From a storage receptacle for dry ice, Plunkett withdrew a cylinder of what should have been freon, but nothing was in the cylinder. His curiosity piqued, Plunkett chose to investigate further. While another person might have believed that the cylinder simply had leaked, and discarded it, Plunkett weighed the cylinder, shook it, and then sliced it open.

He recorded his findings in a notebook: "A white, solid material was obtained, which was supposed to be a polymerized product" of the freon compound. Since the chemical composition was not known, the new product was given a laboratory code number: K-416.

Plunkett's failed experiment in refrigeration would become one of the great scientific success stories of the century. His discovery would produce dividends for the next sixty years.

The substance, white and waxy in nature, would be dubbed polytetrafluoroethylene or PTFE. Now, it is best known under its trademark name of Teflon. Today, Teflon-coated pots, pans, cookie sheets, and muffin tins are an essential component of kitchens in many parts of the world.

Between 75 and 80 percent of the pots and pans sold in the United States are coated with Teflon or a similar material, according to industry estimates.

The substance Plunkett had discovered had some astounding qualities. Teflon is distinguished by its complete indifference to attack by chemicals and its slippery surface. It is able to keep its physical properties over a wide range of temperatures. Heat can pass through Teflon without melting it. Teflon holds together in a vacuum, making it invaluable for use in the space program.

As a result, Teflon has become one of the most valuable and versatile substances ever discovered, contributing to significant advances in such areas as aerospace, communications, electronics, and architecture.

Dr. Roy Plunkett (right) participates in a reenactment of the discovery of Teflon at DuPont's Chambers Works in Deepwater, Salem County.
PHOTOGRAPH COURTESY OF HAGLEY MUSEUM AND LIBRARY

Teflon coats electrical wires, chemical tanks, jogging suits, and light bulbs. Teflon also can be found in some unlikely places. It's been used as a corrosion insulator between the copper skin and inner stainless steel framework of the Statue of Liberty and as a coating for the ten-acre Fiberglass roof of the Silverdome in Pontiac, Michigan.

Teflon's slippery nature made it, well . . . slip into common English usage. Colorado Representative Pat Schroeder dubbed President Reagan the "Teflon president" in 1983 for his ability to deflect blame for problems in his administration. Mob boss John Gotti was known as the "Teflon don" for evading the law several times before finally being convicted.

All of this was far from Plunkett's mind in 1938. A resident of Woodstown, Salem County, Plunkett was only two years out of gradu-ate school—he received a doctorate in chemistry from Ohio State Uni-versity—when he made his discovery.

"If there was any luck involved in the discovery," Plunkett once observed, "probably part of it was that we didn't get blown up."

Plunkett received a patent for his discovery in 1941. Initially, with the United States immersed in World War II, the development of Teflon was limited to government defense work.

In the early stages of the creation of the atomic bomb, Teflon played a key role in proving that atomic fission, the splitting of atoms, was feasible. Teflon was the only gasket material that could contain the corrosive hexafluoride used in making uranium 235 for the bomb.

After the war ended, new peacetime uses for Teflon were developed. In France, Marc Gregoire was the first person to come up with the idea of spreading Teflon over metal to develop nonstick cookware. In May 1956, a store in Paris offered the first Teflon-lined pan for sale, and the world of cooking was changed forever.

Across the Atlantic, DuPont took notice of this new use for the material and began developing its own brand of Teflon cookware. It went on the market in 1962, and the new cookware quickly supplanted the aluminum and stainless steel pots and pans that were commonly used at the time.

DuPont initially promoted its Teflon line by noting that people could cook without applying butter, oil, or other fats to the bottom of the pan. That idea did not take hold with consumers. It was not until DuPont began running television advertisements touting the cookware's easy cleanup that sales began to take off. Sales have been so successful over the years that more than one billion pieces of nonstick cookware have been sold.

The question has been asked: If nothing sticks to Teflon, how does Teflon stick to the pan? It does so through a primer technology developed by DuPont. Nonstick finishes are applied in layers. The first layer is the primer, and it is the special surface chemistry in the primer that makes it adhere to the metal surfaces of the cookware.

Today, DuPont produces a variety of nonstick surfaces for use on cookware. The Teflon coatings can withstand temperatures up to 500 degrees Fahrenheit.

Teflon's application has been refined and improved since it was first introduced. The biggest change has been the introduction of SilverStone nonstick coating in 1976. SilverStone was designed to improve performance and durability.

New uses continue to be discovered. A Japanese company developed an electric rice cooker coated with Teflon in 1993, an innovation that had widespread use in countries where rice is a staple of the daily diet.

Teflon has gone well beyond revolutionizing cooking. During the Apollo space flights of the late 1960s and early 1970s, Teflon was an essential part of the technology that helped us land on the moon. The material coated the outer layers of spacesuits and lined the systems used to carry liquid oxygen. Additional uses for Teflon in space included heat shields for rocket and satellite reentry and wire insulation.

In 1976, Robert Gore, who worked in the wire-coating business, found that a piece of stretched Teflon had tiny holes big enough to let water vapor out, but too small to allow water droplets in. He applied the Teflon to fabric and called it Gore-Tex, the first breathable waterproof clothing.

Gore-Tex is also used in the medical field to remove bacteria and dust during surgical procedures. Teflon itself has been injected into the vocal cords of people who have lost their voices because of extreme vocal cord relaxation. Teflon acts as an inert substance that fills out the cords, allowing people to use their voices again.

Today, the most extensive use of Teflon is in the electronics industry. Telephone and computer cables are insulated with Teflon because of its resistance to fire.

After his discovery, Plunkett stayed with DuPont until his retirement in 1975. His importance to science was duly recognized. Plunkett was inducted into the Plastics Hall of Fame in 1973, then into the National Inventors Hall of Fame in 1985, putting him in the company of Thomas Edison and the Wright Brothers.

Plunkett died of cancer on May 12, 1994, leaving a legacy of involvement with a discovery that "is as important to modern society as the light bulb, telephone, and automobile," as one DuPont executive put it in 1988.

Plunkett summed up his feelings that same year, on the occasion of the anniversary of his discovery of Teflon: "I've had a good career, a good life," he said. "I enjoyed my work all the time. I got to associate with top people. So I can't say I want to do my life over, because I don't think that it could have been any better if I did." Certainly, grateful cooks around the world would agree.

LEISURE & RECREATION

Point in Time

Their ship loomed just offshore in the twilight, as they brought their bounty onto the beach: bulging sacks of coin of the realm, trunks of jewels. Inland they trudged, in search of a cove, a boulder, a hillside. Shovels at the ready.

This terrain, at the very tip of a British colony whose imperial bosses rarely ventured beyond their civilized boundaries, provided a suitable layover for Captain William Kidd and his corps. He had spied a lake nearby and knew his briny boys would have fresh water. Through the mist, the skull-and-crossbones caught the moon's early light. And the treasure disappeared into the night.

The dunes rise like a fortress protecting this storybook village by the sea. Thick with grass and bayberry bushes, they rim the beachfront overlooking the juncture of the Atlantic Ocean and Delaware Bay.

Landward, tree-shaded streets radiate from the town "circle" embroidered with colorful flower beds. In summer, foliage hides most of tongue-shaped Lily Lake, where the birth of eight cygnets one Mother's Day not long ago sent mama swan and the Cape May Point populace into a tizzy of maternalism.

Moving from lake to beachfront, anglers challenge the surf, and distant boats dot the horizon. The world of cares and conflict is but a rumor. Life is as huggable as a beach ball.

At this nub of shoreline—the southernmost point in New Jersey—the riches are largely peace and quiet.

The open-air pavilion was packed with twenty-five hundred Presbyterians gathered to debate matters of morality and temperance. In 1875, America's evangelical fervor was at full throttle, and a town called Sea Grove had just been chartered at the southern tip of the New Jersey peninsula. Six years later, the pavilion was gone, and other religions had discovered the now incorporated and renamed borough of Cape May Point. The first of several churches to find a home here was St. Peter's Episcopal, which began its life as a small exhibit building at the 1876 Centennial in Philadelphia.

The nineteenth-century Point held commercial as well as spiritual promise. The Shoreham Hotel provided lodgers with a dramatic ocean view for two dollars a day, and promoters extolled its "refined patronage." Aside Lake Lily, one-time water hole of the notorious Captain Kidd, the country-club lodge sat on a knoll and boat hulls littered the lawn. Ladies in long, white, summer dresses strolled across the rustic bridge that spanned the lake; others reached from rowboats for the lilies that carpeted the water. At night, boaters glided by lantern light, and the lake sparkled like a fairyland.

Travelers arrived by steamship at what is now Sunset Beach, on the bay and just beyond borough limits. The Ocean Street Passenger Railway transported visitors to town, where Philadelphia merchant John Wanamaker and President Benjamin Harrison's wife maintained summer residences. Advertisements claimed that the Point was paradise and "cooler than Cape May."

Rocking chairs still sway on the block-long porches, but the ballroom has become a chapel, as the Shoreham is now St. Mary-by-the-Sea, a retreat for an order of Catholic sisters. Boats no longer crease the lake, the bridge is gone, the lilies are sparse, and the trolleys have disappeared. The streets are a mix of cottages and contemporaries, screened porches and sweeping decks, the sleek and the stately. Change visits all locales, but some resist a change of heart. Cape May Point remains a refuge for the nerves, a neighborhood paced by yesterday's values.

In the 1990s, the post office was still equipped with a canceling machine, which imprinted the borough name, and dated to a time when Wanamaker, one of the town founders, was postmaster general of the United States.

On the same block, the historic Wanamaker cottage bears the stamp of another of the town's religious orders: the Marianists, who hold a series of one-week family retreats that make summer an active time here. Catty-corner to the Marianists' house stands a startling Victorian that locals call the Gray Ghost. Busy with gables and balusters, its bluish-gray hue nearly matches the ocean's.

Though ghosts inhabit all coastal towns, living landmarks are more accessible. One such site here is an Ocean Avenue guest house, where a walk through the lush gardens is more calming than any tranquilizer. Formerly a home for young women established by Philadelphia social-ite Mary J. Drexel, the guest house is aptly named Somewhere in Time.

Set on a triangular lot enclosed by a white picket fence, St. Peter's-by-the-Sea is a testament to stamina and serenity. A quartet of clergy-men had the building shipped here in 1879, and it has been moved four times since. The salt air wages a constant assault, but inside, the south-ern yellow pine paneling looks like new.

And in Pavilion Circle Park, the shouting comes not from pro-nouncements of probity, but from teenagers dueling at the volleyball net.

Yet the ghosts of pirates are never far from this placid locale vulner-able to another type of plunder.

There was once a Beach Avenue in Cape May Point, but the ocean claimed it and parts of two other streets a century ago. Geography has made the Point both blessed and precarious. After the powerful 1991 Halloween storm, about one-third of the borough was underwater. The state funded drainage work and reconstruction of dune fencing, bulkheads, and beach staircases. Battling the elements is seashore reality.

That sense of vulnerability seems removed from the gazebo at Mayor Malcolm Fraser's Lake Drive home, which is more country manor than seashore dwelling. But the unpredictable tides are never far away, and Fraser knows well the price of vigilance. He remembers walking the beach right into Cape May years ago, but that strand has since been scooped away, and other Point beaches face the constant specter of erosion. In addition, threats to drinking water throughout the environmentally fragile Cape are a source of constant concern and close observation.

Indeed, reminders of a darker, violent world contrast starkly with the trusting cheerfulness that is Cape May Point. On Sunset Boulevard, part of which borders the borough, an observation tower that scanned the seas for German U-boats during World War II looms over cyclists and motorists. An ominous concrete bunker, whose big guns were set to fire on those stealthy subs, sits on the beach along with the rusted bases of wartime radio towers. Remnants of another siege—the War of 1812—are seen a few blocks away; the jagged planks and driftwood form the skeleton of a gunboat that met a fiery demise as it blockaded the bay.

Other sites tell a different story. The great lighthouse, whose beacon saved many a distressed mariner, towers over the state park in Lower Township just outside the borough line. Nestled in a tangle of trees off the roadway is the Cape May Bird Observatory, an ally to species threatened by loss of habitat. In summer, not far from the lighthouse, feeding porpoises leap and dive in the ocean.

Captain Kidd should have stayed put here—when he sailed north, he was captured in New York, dispatched across the Atlantic, and tried and hanged in England in 1701.

Today, Cape May Point still means safe harbor. Unconquered by the ocean's fury or a flighty society, it remains fixed somewhere in time.

Before Gambling Was Legal

Dutchy's second-floor casino embraced the seduction of a Saturday night. Roulette players stood transfixed before the wheel's hypnotic spin. Dice skittered across the craps tables. Poker faces eyed poker hands, while faro dealers drew and dared.

Outdoors, far removed from the vertiginous clamor, the ocean heaved and rolled, a sure bet every time. As always, Atlantic City's scenic charms competed with its synthetic diversions. Gambling remained a high-profile, high-stakes enterprise in the nineties.

The 1890s.

Irony. It is the byword of modern times, the change-up that reality tosses us—sometimes gentle, sometimes fierce, always instructive.

The Atlantic City seascape's inevitably ironic undertow is perfectly illustrated by the town's gambling history. Things have rarely been

The ship-shaped bar at Babette's, a nightclub–gambling den from the 1920s to the 1940s, lubricated high rollers and the high-toned.
IMAGE COURTESY COLLECTION OF VICKI GOLD LEVI

what they appeared to be. The Brighton Casino (at the long vanished Brighton Hotel), for example, featured a ballroom, bowling alley, solarium, and swimming pool—not a gaming table in sight. Patrons of Dutchy Muhlrod's high-end (five and ten dollars per bet) establishment on Delaware Avenue, their blood running hot even when their luck grew cold, discounted one mildly irritating technicality: gambling was illegal.

Dutchy's crowd was in fast company, as gaming rooms proliferated in late nineteenth-century Atlantic City. Nickel-limit joints dominated Mississippi Avenue. An Arkansas Avenue house run by one Charles Coleman served up craps games to hotel waiters. Harry Smith's saloon–gambling den prospered on Baltic Avenue. In a celebrated case, an executive of the National Cash Register Company claimed that an Arctic Avenue emporium plied him with drink and freed his wallet of five hundred dollars—no small change in those days. The city prosecutor identified sixteen local gambling "dives," but prosecution proved elusive.

It had always been so (and would always be), though Civil War–era mayor Lewis Reed quashed a dicey operation when he responded to a resident's complaint about a "shanty where gamblers made rendezvous." Yes, gambling was indigenous to Atlantic City virtually from the start, when the Camden and Atlantic Railroad brought its first batch of city dwellers to Absecon Island in 1854. The liberating scent of salt air, the impulse to challenge taboos, and the carnivorous grasp of the pitchman all fostered an atmosphere of distraction and devilment. The sand, sea, and recreational bonanza provided clean, invigorating romps, but when the sun slipped below the ocean rim, pulses danced to a different instinct. Gambling was the grease that coated the city's dark side and slicked the palms of the powerbrokers. Ultimately, it dictated the region's economy.

"Atlantic City couldn't have survived without [gambling]," said Grace D'Amato, sister-in-law of the late Paul "Skinny" D'Amato, whose famed 500 Club offered premium entertainment and cloaked its gambling parlor within earshot of the stage. "It was a paradox—it was illegal, but wide open."

The worst-kept secret in town, insiders told outsiders. In the 1920s, as mobsters strolled Atlantic City's "neutral" surf, Stebbins's Golden Inn at Mississippi and Pacific avenues combined bootlegged liquor with games of chance. When Daniel Stebbins, who sported the cleancut looks of a Miss America Pageant host, married showgirl Blanche Babbitt, he christened the club Babette's (after his bride's stage name), charcoaled steaks imported from Chicago, and filled the stage with leggy dancers. Behind the club's porthole windows, furs and politicos mixed with racetrack refugees at the backroom tables. The beefiest boss of them all—Al Capone—paid a visit. For quick getaways, a trapdoor from the "horse room" led to steps that climbed to the roof, where another stairway descended to the sanctuary of Stebbins's home.

Escape was seldom a necessity, however, as the authorities winked at—and profited from—local gambling operations. GOP boss Enoch L. "Nucky" Johnson, treasurer of Atlantic County and King of the Rackets, controlled the city from his headquarters at the Ritz-Carlton Hotel. Gambling was as protected as a duned beach, and Johnson presided as a benevolent despot.

"Virtually every nightclub had gambling," said Grace D'Amato. "But there was no violence—everyone got along. . . . It was a way of life."

D'Amato especially remembers the Hialeah Club (Atlantic Avenue between Michigan and Ohio), the Clicquot Club (Illinois Avenue), and, of course, the 500 Club, where her husband, Emil "Willie" D'Amato, joined older brother Skinny at what became a Missouri Avenue landmark. Skinny had begun his career while a teenager, launching a cigar shop–cum–gambling joint at Arctic and Missouri, then opening a similar establishment at Columbia Place and Pacific Avenue, before eventually landing the post of casino manager at Luigi's Restaurant (Arkansas and Pacific), owned by boyhood chum Jake "Colby" Berenato. When 500 Club founder Phil Barr died in 1942, Skinny bought into the club and soon became sole owner. The "Fives" was the first venue to pair Dean Martin and Jerry Lewis, and, in later years, Sinatra swung before packed houses. Meanwhile, two small, draped gambling rooms behind the bar hosted the postshow action.

Another side of town also brimmed with nightlife and freewheeling gambling. Entertainment mecca Club Harlem, on Kentucky Avenue near Arctic, offered an assortment of table games in a thirty-by-forty-foot room entered through an open doorway aside the front bar.

"The money was piled as high as your head," said Sid Trusty, a drummer and bandleader at Club Harlem for three decades. "There were guys in tuxes—it was high class."

Elsewhere, the dress was plainer and the lights dimmer, but the betting just as active. Trusty, who later stockpiled African-American memorabilia at his Ohio Avenue home, recalled a large casino in Venice Park (overlooking the bay at the end of Ohio Avenue) and a horse room complete with chalkboard in the Timbuktu, a busy bar at North Carolina and Atlantic avenues. Wagering on card games was commonplace in bars, rooming houses, and pool halls, where a vacant table also invited dice shooters. "It was small money, but the house would take a cut," said Trusty, who, moonlighting as a cabdriver, shuttled many card sharks to their appointed games. "People had to do things to make money to exist. . . . Of course, they had to take care of the cop on the beat, too."

Sometimes, though, law enforcement showed up at the door with an ax instead of an outstretched hand. On those occasions, headlines were sure to follow.

The detectives approached the three-story house, bone-colored in the moonlight. Skirting plump sedans parked at curbside, they stepped onto the awninged veranda and knocked at the door. Curtains parted, muffled words were exchanged, and the door opened. The newcomers were led through an anteroom past the well-stocked kitchen to a second floor of fluorescent light, piled carpeting, and draperies hugging venetian blinds. Sharpies eyed the wheel, while dice tumbled on the felt.

Forty people were arrested that night—actually, in the wee small hours of an August morning in 1958—and taken by bus to the hoosegow, where they were charged as "inmates of a gambling house." The authorities also removed from circulation several roulette wheels and nineteen thousand dollars in hard cash. The Bath and Turf Club on the boardwalk block of Iowa Avenue—in the shadow of Nucky Johnson's beloved Ritz, no less—was out of commission.

For the time being.

The state had orchestrated this bust, following a period of surveillance ordered by the attorney general, who had been tipped off by mail. The gambling setup had been in operation for less than a week.

But the Bath and Turf had long been a prime gambling spot, with recurring games enjoying laissez faire or staying a step ahead of the law. Eighteen years earlier, a raid here had discovered gambling equipment but no practitioners—the gamblers had hightailed it out of harm's way. It was the era of Mayor Tommy "Two-Guns" Taggart, who packed a pair of pistols and vowed to clean up the town, as the U.S. Army turned it into a training base during World War II. (Ironically, Taggart was a protege of Nucky Johnson, but all was fair in vice and war.)

Taggart's posse of night raiders, spearheaded by a quartet of off-duty cops called the Four Horsemen, brought many a high roller to heel. The county sheriff grabbed a share of the spotlight in a 1943 raid at Babette's, arresting proprietor Stebbins and seizing roulette wheels, craps tables, and racing sheets. Meanwhile, other rackets also were closed by the roundup. Atlantic City's Wild West had been tamed.

For the time being.

Babette's reportedly recovered in short order. After the war, as the soldiers departed, the hotels resumed regular operations and so did the gambling parlors. While the country cleaved to the suburbanizing, sometimes puritanical fifties, Las Vegas flourished and Atlantic City debated the slippery issue of public morality. A movement to legalize gambling on the island gained press attention in March 1958—within months of the raid at the Bath and Turf. Strangely enough, the effort received strong support from the Atlantic City Chamber of Commerce Women's Division, the Gold Star Mothers of Atlantic County, and the Seashore Hairdressers Union, among other women's groups. The law remained unyielding, but the debate would resonate with a new generation two decades later.

As early as 1905, opponents had sought to eradicate the nefarious pastime in South Atlantic City (now Margate), and succeeded in shutting down at least one establishment. Nearly half a century later, a May 1952 foray uncovered thirty thousand dollars' worth of "numbers" slips stacked in paper bags on the dining room table of a Coolidge Avenue bungalow. Atlantic City Detective Captain Jerry Sullivan and his Cleanup Squad made the bust; the principals were charged with "aiding and abetting a lottery."

Indeed, while backroom gambling parlors hosted big-dollar games, numbers running was a cottage industry for the small-time bettor, who could win five dollars for a penny wager. Bettors recorded three-digit numbers on slips of paper, which runners picked up and relayed to a drop site, where low-level racketeers decided whether to lay off some of the heavier bets on bigger operators. The winning numbers often were indexed to specified daily horse races at various tracks, and players scrambled to check the late editions of the local papers to learn their fate. "Every corner store wrote numbers," said Sid Trusty.

And just about every grocery store had a slot machine, and there were home-based bookies for assorted sporting events, according to Grace D'Amato, who also recalled a Margate neighbor who booked numbers and "made a nice living."

Slot machines jangled at locations as diverse as Margate's Anglers Club of Absecon Island (an aging writer remembers his grandmother flush with coins, while hard-bitten anglers lost their bait money) and the storied Atlantic City Country Club in Northfield, where they loomed large in the genesis of the Atlantic City Race Course.

As related in local author William E. Kelly's Atlantic City Country Club history, *Birth of the Birdie*, club president Sonny Fraser and several fellow members (including Philadelphia builder John B. Kelly) formed the Atlantic City Racing Association in a bid to bring thoroughbred racing to the southern New Jersey Shore. The country club's half-dozen nickel, dime, and quarter machines ruffled regulators and threatened final approval of the racetrack. Ultimately, the slots stayed, but Sonny Fraser was supplanted by older brother Leo as ACCC president, clearing the way for the track.

When the state police, who staged an annual golf outing at the Northfield club, informed Leo Fraser of an impending crackdown on illegal gambling in the early 1950s, the slots went into storage.

Relics of another day, these slot machines likely were built by Bally Manufacturing, then the industry heavyweight, and now, as Bally Entertainment Corporation, a part of giant Hilton Hotels Corporation, which has added the Atlantic City Country Club to its empire. The world has changed. Atlantic City's smoky, surreptitious gambling dens have yielded to glittering casinos built for the masses and backed by corporate muscle. They are breathtaking in scale, profitable, and legal.

The Big Wheel

The Pittsburgh engineer smoothed his luxuriant mustache as he watched the wooden wheel spinning skyward on the boardwalk between Atlantic City's New York and Kentucky avenues. Scrubbed and dirty-faced youths crammed the boxlike seats, eager for stomach flutters. Men plunked down their nickels at the gate. Women passed regally, billowing dresses brushing the boardwalk.

They were all about to ride the latest in a centuries-old line of "pleasure wheels" powered by our enduring fascination with circular motion.

This sixteen-seat "Observation Roundabout" was the creation of local impresario William Somers (of the family that founded Somers Point). The name of the cagy, mustachioed observer from western Pennsylvania was George Washington Gale Ferris. The year was 1891, the world was young, and ideas were there for the taking.

Two years later, the planners of Chicago's Columbian Exposition sought a landmark to rival the Eiffel Tower, built for the Paris Exposition of 1889, and G.W.G. Ferris seized the day. His revolutionary specifications detailed how a giant, steel wheel could be erected based

The 140-foot-high Ferris wheel at Ocean City's Wonderland Pier dominates the skyline.
PHOTOGRAPH BY ELIZABETH WILK

on the same engineering principles applied to bridge construction, principles that assured proper tension and support. His blueprint called for a wheel 250 feet in diameter buttressed by two 140-foot towers and steadied by an inner wheel and a steel spider web of rods and girders connected to the hub. A 1,000-horsepower steam engine would drive the apparatus, enabling forty people at a sitting to ride in each of three dozen trolleylike cars.

Suddenly, building an amusement ride was like building a dam or a canal. Amusements were about to enter the machine age.

Ferris was awarded the contract despite some doubt that his monster wheel could stay upright. As the Chicago winter took hold, construction crews dug foundations, built scaffolding, and grappled with thousands of special parts shipped by rail. The wheel's huge axle (forty-six feet long, thirty-three inches in diameter, and weighing more than forty-six tons) was, at the time, the largest piece of steel ever fashioned in the United States.

By late June, the wheel was complete, a dazzling revolving testament to guts and geometry. Men in straw hats and women in long dresses walked up a balustraded staircase and onto the great wheel for its maiden turn. Thousands weighted to the ground gazed in wonder.

One spectator who was less than delighted was William Somers.

He had bid for the concession at the Expo, but had been rejected. Now he stood outside the fairgrounds, keeping company with his double-wheel roundabout. He had brought the contraption to Chicago to siphon away some business from Ferris and to make a statement—one that, he hoped, might have some legal ramifications. Somers had a patent on his ride's drive mechanism—essentially a rope that fit in a groove around the edge of the wooden wheel. Ferris, however, used a different drive mechanism, one that consisted of a series of cogs bolted onto a chain that ran between two pulleys. The differing drive and the larger wheel's unique superstructure formed the basis of a ruling in a subsequent lawsuit (brought by Somers) that patent infringement had not occurred.

And that is why the graceful ride is not universally known today as the Somers Wheel.

Steeplechase Pier

Squinting into the twilight, the sheriff leaned over the Atlantic City boardwalk railing and spat a plug of tobacco onto the sands. Trickery was afoot—he could smell it. The object of his surveillance was one Pauline Hall, an operetta singer (a "coveted goddess of song," the newspapers proclaimed) scheduled to perform in town that evening.

The question was where? Miss Hall had signed contracts with two venues for the same date, and though one of them—the established Academy of Music at the boardwalk and New York Avenue—had obtained an injunction prohibiting her from appearing elsewhere, the law suspected an end run.

Despite his vigilance, the sheriff was primed to be hoodwinked. As he scanned the boards, two muscular men carried a steamer trunk across the beach below, up a makeshift walkway, and through a side entrance of the brand-new Auditorium Pier. Sardined inside the trunk was the dauntless Hall, who had agreed to headline the pier's maiden show originally scheduled for three weeks earlier. But a dispute between developers and the city over pier length had postponed opening night, prompting the singer to ink another pact. Now Auditorium was ready to rock, and Hall made her choice: she would warble in the new digs.

That was the way of things the first week of August 1899, as growth-minded Atlantic City anticipated the new century with bold vision and a dab of larceny. Auditorium Pier, a profusion of spires and arched windows, extended a thousand feet oceanward from the boardwalk between Pennsylvania and North Carolina avenues, just beyond wide-shouldered Haddon Hall. Its mission was to provide seaside grace, musical entertainment, and "refined vaudeville," but a dramatic personality change was in store. Auditorium Pier would soon metamorphose into Steeplechase–the Funny Place, mecca for clowns and commoners, whips and whirlpools, low-rent rides and high-pitched thrills.

The transformation came quickly. A five-man combine had built Auditorium Pier after leasing the land underneath it from owners William Riddle and Joseph Brady. Two years after its opening, the pier was in receivership. Enter entrepreneur extraordinaire George Cornelius Tilyou, the man who had invented Coney Island, launched his career by selling bottles of sand and saltwater to midwestern tourists, and been captivated by George Ferris's huge, revolving wheel at the 1893 Columbian Exposition in Chicago. Tilyou erected his own Ferris wheel at Coney and surrounded it with Steeplechase Park, named for its ride that simulated the rugged equestrian event. When he took over Atlantic City's Auditorium Pier, however, Tilyou retained a lineup of bands and minstrel shows . . . at first. He hired renowned bandmaster composer John Philip Sousa to fill the salt air with stirring sounds but bristled when most people marched right onto the beach and caught the concert for free. So in 1904, Tilyou scrapped the music and converted the pier into an amusement emporium. Renaming it was a simple matter.

Steeplechase slapped on the greasepaint and turned a funny face toward seashore visitors. The boardwalk entrance assumed the contours of a giant clown's open mouth. Large lettering on the side of the pier announced "The Mirth Place of the Nation" and "A Playground of Innocent Amusement for Young and Old."

Indeed, for those with stable stomachs and no fear of heights, a bevy of rides offered beguiling diversion with a dash of titillation. At the ocean end of the pier, the Ferris wheel spun lazily toward the heavens. A hundred feet across the deck, seats dangled on towering chains and twirled dizzy riders above a groaning platform. The Human Roulette Wheel (later the Whirlpool) spilled brave souls down a long, steep chute onto a banked, circular vortex of polished wood; escape was improbable, slip-sliding inevitable. Clown costumes were available for those with a flair for symbolism.

The Funny Place made people laugh, and spectators invariably became participants. Corporate America was quick to spot the correlation between mirth and money, and up went the big signs: Texaco above the ocean pavilion, Wrigley's overlooking the beach, and in 1926, the 215 foot-long Chesterfield extravaganza of 26,000 multicolored light bulbs—the largest electric sign in the world.

But the majestic cigarette sign went up in smoke on February 14, 1932, when the entire frame structure was ravaged by a fire that started at the boardwalk end. The rides became charred wrecks; the great Ferris wheel collapsed and disappeared into the ocean. At the front of the pier, a florist shop, an ice cream parlor, and four other stores were destroyed.

Fire was no stranger to the wooden amusement parks of yesteryear—a blaze had claimed Coney Island's Steeplechase Park nearly three decades earlier, and George C. Tilyou had promptly rebuilt. The Great Man was gone by the time Steeplechase Pier toppled, but eldest son, Edward, shared his father's conviction that the show never stops. By July 1932, a new pier was rising from the ashes. Steeplechase reopened the following year, shorter and plainer, but packed with more attractions than before: the sharp-eyed barkers and their carnival games, the Hell Hole promising unrelieved fright, the daring Tilt-a-Whirl producing screams and an agreeable disorientation, the Whip with its coachlike seats alternately gliding and lurching along rails enclosed by a picket fence.

Right after World War II, when gasoline was scarce and spirits were high, Steeplechase became a magnet for families and boardwalk strollers, and a rendezvous for ex-servicemen in uniform and young women wearing flared skirts—some local historians say that this period was the pier's heyday. In the seemingly untrammeled 1950s, the rides hummed and youthful shrieks thinned into chirps across a broad expanse of beach dotted with cabanas.

At Steeplechase Pier, the laughs and screams of delight formed a chorus over the ocean.
PHOTOGRAPH COURTESY OF THE *COURIER-POST*

In 1967, Steeplechase added a roller coaster and, two years later, a mountainous slide, but innocence was fast receding from the Shore. As the town changed its profile, Atlantic City's other storied piers died or reinvented themselves, but Steeplechase clung to its straw-hat simplicity. Resorts International paid two million dollars in stock to acquire the property in 1982, then closed the pier four years later.

Fire struck once more. On December 10, 1988, as funnyman Dom DeLuise readied for his evening show across the boardwalk at Resorts, an eight-hour conflagration leveled the Funny Place yet again. Years later, its skeleton remained, lapped by the immutable surf.

Today's world is both more sophisticated and more precarious than the one enlivened by George C. Tilyou and the impresarios of the Gilded Age. At the seashore, sleek has displaced quaint, and coastal development is often subjected to a roller coaster of red tape.

But there's a certain something about a pier, isn't there? Something timeless and romantic and childlike; the sway of the pilings, the rush of water below.

And so there are persistent dreams that the old structures will be reborn, that someday a new pier will rise at North Carolina and the boardwalk. Indeed, drawing-board plans appear now and then, and in the late 1990s, federal and state environmental agencies issued permits authorizing reconstruction.

It is our impulse to retrieve the past, our enduring homage to the barker's cry, the seductive sheen of a carny game under moonlight, the whole whirling transport that was Steeplechase.

Yes, a pier—the mere idea of a pier—still grabs us. A place to stroll, sit, snack, inhale the sea breeze, and gaze at the fathomless ocean. Funny, but true.

Garden Pier

T he pier glistened at nighttime. A colonnade of lampposts lit the way to the ocean, and the illuminated theater loomed castlelike in the moon's cloud-filtered gaze. Inside, the dance instructor laid down a flurry of tango steps. He was nocturnal, sinuous, a study in black, all fierce eyes and Mediterranean allure. He had his fans. Female fans.

"Now, you try," the instructor said to his charges, gathered round in a semicircle. The class shuffled into position and waited for his command. The Victrola played, the instructor led, the ladies followed. When he accelerated, they strained to keep pace, some gasping at their own exertions and the marvel of their teacher's effortlessness. And the cut of his black pants.

The music stopped and his smile shot across the floorboards, his arms stretched toward the vaulted ceiling. "You are all stars," said the instructor, known only as Monsieur Rudolph.

Tango teacher-turned-matinee idol Rudolph Valentino soon became the brightest star in the firmament—for a while.

Atlantic City's Garden Pier, a top boardwalk attraction in the 1920s, yielded to the brittle fate that bedeviled most of its peers, but has found new life as the city's repository of seashore lore and historical lure.

In the beginning, the seaward structure was intent on making its own history. When theater impresario George H. Earle sold a row of boardwalk stores to Philadelphia meatpackers Alfred and Louis Burk in 1912, six major piers already creased the Atlantic City surf. Ironically, it was the brothers Burk—not fellow Philadelphian Earle—who had the show biz bug, as they formed the Pier Holding and Realty Company and hired the architectural firm of Simon and Bassett to design Absecon Island's seventh pier, just east of New Jersey Avenue.

The specifications called for twenty-five stores, a courtyard flanked by parallel pavilions, and a four-towered edifice complete with ballroom, theater, and exhibition hall. Directly across the boardwalk from Hotel Rudolf (no connection to Valentino), the first Garden Pier, seven hundred feet in length, was dedicated in January 1913. Five years later, vaudeville king B. F. Keith set up shop here, hosting the shenanigans of Fanny Brice and Eddie Cantor, while dueling the rapacious Shubert Brothers for available talent. John Philip Sousa struck up the band; Gypsy Rose Lee peeled off her gloves. Musicals and legit theater came on board, but the popular taste was fickle—halfway through an opening-night performance of *The Student Prince*, the audience stopped the show, insisting that leading man De Wolfe Hopper recite his classic "Casey at the Bat." The curtain closed, Hopper stepped in front and completed his familiar rendition, and there was joy in Mudville . . . or, at least, at the Garden Pier.

Paul Whiteman's orchestra swung on Sunday afternoons, presaging the Big Band Era, when the likes of Maestro Fletcher Henderson and crooner Rudy Vallee filled the salt air with smooth sounds. Indoor golf, a children's carnival, and a kennel club claimed space on the marquee, as courtyard planters blossomed into lush flower beds, creating the Garden Pier's distinctive look, accented by shrubs, gazebos, a pond, and a small countrified bridge across a stream. Flags rippled atop the Keith Theatre's quartet of steeples and terra-cotta roof, as striped awnings shaded arched entranceways below. Artists propped their wares on easels to catch the public eye. Nothing could compromise this nineteenth-century-style ambience—not even the ramp that ushered Packards and Hudsons to subboardwalk parking.

Indoors or out, Garden Pier reflected a sense of showmanship. In 1916, a fourteen-ton Underwood typewriter moved into the company's "Products and Progress" pavilion, and kids sat on key tabs big as stools at a soda fountain. The Underwood "Standard"—1,728 times normal size—was fully operational, typing copy (on rather large paper) via remote control. It wowed patrons at Garden Pier for eighteen years and closed its career at Convention Hall before being scrapped during World War II.

Five years after the Underwood behemoth arrived, the Pier hosted an event typecast for Atlantic City. The maiden Inter-City Bathing Beauty Contest assembled eight hopefuls before the judges' scrutiny at the Keith Theatre, and a wee lass named Margaret Gorman captured top honors. In subsequent years, the contest became a pageant, and the pageant an icon: Miss America.

Other performers seized the spotlight with guts rather than grace. Encased in a straitjacket, death-defying Harry Houdini dangled from the heights of the Keith Theatre—the master illusionist never failed to attract a gaping and gasping crowd with his signature stunt. Then there was the flagpole sitter who stayed aloft to avoid a domestic summons, his angry wife and the constable poised below.

Yes, Garden Pier was a true showplace. But it quickly became more white elephant than cash cow, as the bigger piers with their frenetic amusements grabbed the crowds. By 1929, the adjacent Hotel Rudolf having grown into the majestic Breakers, Garden Pier owners entertained outside plans to build an eleven-story hotel on the pier, but the city blocked the bid. Appeals reached the Supreme Court in a case that would resonate a generation later.

The property changed hands in 1932, and by the end of the decade, theater productions had dwindled. The new ownership was fragmented and absentee; the pier sagged as delinquent taxes mounted. Finally, the city foreclosed in 1944, as that year's monster hurricane took an additional toll, though it left the pier intact. A planned public sale evaporated in the face of legal uncertainty, and indeed, one of the local conundrums of the late 1940s was "what to do about the Garden Pier?"

Prospects were complicated by the federal government's claim—based on the earlier Supreme Court opinion—that the United States was the rightful owner of all pier structures oceanward of the "low-water mark." Meanwhile, the owners of record were seeking a break for payment of back taxes.

It was low tide at the Garden Pier, but after several rounds of litigation, the city gained title to the property, demolished the superstructures, and levied a luxury tax to fund the pier's reconstruction. On July 3, 1954, timed to celebrate the Atlantic City Centennial, the new Garden Pier greeted the public. The look was *moderne*: squared-off pavilion wings, flower beds shrunk to patches, a herringbone wooden deck leading to a circular marble fountain fronting a smooth-masonry band shell. The bandstand faced the ocean and an outdoor amphitheater

High suspense: Harry Houdini performed his famous escape act while dangling from the heights of the Garden Pier, circa 1917.

PHOTOGRAPH COURTESY COLLECTION OF VICKI GOLD LEVI

that had displaced the gaudy Keith Theatre and its trappings of vaude-ville—now the fare was to be symphonic, operatic, big bold sounds under an awning of daytime sky or a canvas of stars.

For the Centennial concert, the mayor slashed ribbons, an Ameri-can Legion band played red-white-and-blue, and a crowd of three thou-sand bulged well beyond the graded seating. In the coming years, there were choral societies, organ concerts, the rousing U.S. Infantry Sym-phonic Band, and a Pittsburgh singing group composed of steel work-ers and called, appropriately, "Voices of Steel."

Solid stuff, and all free. Yet Garden Pier was not all it could be, or what many wanted it to become. A planned aquarium and fishing deck never materialized, and business leaders trying to stimulate uptown commerce bemoaned the pier's "lack of attractions." Though the con-certs continued, and a senior center and modest coastal museum joined an art center established at the outset, foot traffic was slowing.

Soon enough, all the grand piers lost their luster, and Atlantic City sprung a new landscape on both sides of the boardwalk.

The Garden Pier's ancient concrete piles are still there, sunken deep in the ocean floor, charred skeletal remains too stubborn to yield to time or tide. Thick crossbeams lattice the top and wild sea grass grows in the breach. Hovering over the spot where orchestras once poured melody into the summer night, sea gulls screech their own symphony, then glide toward the boardwalk to forage for food.

Today's Garden Pier is a unique package of seashore past and present. The band shell, though empty and silent, still stands. Lime-green gargoyles that commanded the heights of the vanished Marlborough-Blenheim Hotel now adorn the curving fountain that retains its grace and polish. The pier's original configuration persists, with a new pair of sandstone-and-aquamarine wings: on one side, the Atlantic City Art Center, revived after a savage 1981 fire and redesigned in 1994; across the courtyard, now gated, the mirror-image Atlantic City Historical Museum.

Somewhere between the cacophony of the gulls and the mute, or-dered displays is the echo of history.

The Anglers Club

The youngest member ever of The Anglers Club of Absecon Island turned sixteen at a time when the musical strains of Herman's Hermits slipped out of transistor radios on the sand and bikinis overtook the beach in earnest. Mostly, though, he remembers the fishing.

His grandfather, a crackerjack fisherman, secured his berth at the private club in Margate, and he seized the opportunity. He fished at dawn, at night, in the rain, and through dry spells that might have made Hemingway's "Old Man" wince. Fishing, after all, was a man's pastime. Men with leather thumbs that hooks couldn't pierce; men whose stubble peeped through sun-hardened cheeks and who tucked blood-smeared towels under their belts. Meanwhile, their wives played canasta in the clubhouse.

Except for the teenager's grandmother. She could out-fish and, on occasion, out-swear almost any man. Though women and children were consigned to a small fishing area about thirty yards closer to shore than the eighty-foot-wide men's tee at the end of the pier, grandma caught her share of fish. In the off-season, she snuck out front and joined the hard-bitten fraternity. Some grumbled, but most of them loved it.

The membership boasted once prominent executives, doctors, and lawyers, a few celebrities, and more than a few characters. They adopted the young man that summer. Sam Wilen, of Wilen Wines, was a little chatterbox always in motion. Karl Kaufmann, of Kaufmann's Department Stores in Pittsburgh, was silent and ramrod-straight. Dr. Leo Stein, a Philadelphia dentist, liked to brag about his protégé's fishing exploits. Former lightweight boxing contender Lew Tendler, at the time a well-known Atlantic City restaurateur, was a longtime member. So was Sigmund (Sig) Heller, who was approaching his 100th birthday and reputedly had prospected for gold in the Klondike region of Canada before the turn of the century.

Expert angler Salvatore Todaro would keep eyes forever front as he nudged anglers along the rail, maneuvering to snare his catch—nothing could break his concentration. A modest man named Frank Young taught young people how to cast, snap the rod forward, and

Landing the big ones was not uncommon in the early days of The Anglers Club.
PHOTOGRAPH COURTESY OF THE ANGLERS CLUB OF ABSECON ISLAND.

release the line without tangling it. He had a quiet dignity; his strength was in his eyes and forearms.

All were equals before the rod and reel.

For the youngest member, casting was half the fun, the weighted line flying toward the horizon and nearly disappearing before plunking into the sea. He lived for interclub contests, which pitted the Margate anglers against hook-and-liners from Ventnor and Ocean City. Suiting up beside his grandfather in the locker room, he was Mickey Mantle before a World Series game. On went the uniform: official shirt, light sweater, and windbreaker (it could be nippy out over the ocean, even in summer) topped by a cap bearing the club's insignia. Then the gathering of gear—two-piece rods and baskets full of hooks, corks, weights, lures, and jars of bloodworms—and the march down the gangway. Out front, fishermen claimed their spots, and for a moment, there was only the rhythmic sloshing of the ocean. Then, a scratchy but boisterous recording sent the National Anthem winging skyward while a sheet of Stars and Stripes snapped overhead.

It was show time.

In an earlier time, "gentlemen fishermen" stood in the Atlantic City surf every Sunday (even in winter) to participate in casting contests. Aristocratic-looking in bow tie, knickers, and spats, local sportsman H. Willard Shaner eyed the coastline and envisioned a private fishing pier downbeach. He recruited a band of twenty venerable anglers and persuaded the Margate commissioners that the oceanfront between Essex and Douglas avenues was the perfect place for a fishing club. The group sold private bonds to finance the purchase of riparian rights (sixteen thousand dollars) and the construction of the pier (nine thousand dollars). It was the spring of 1923, and The Anglers Club soon extended three hundred feet from the boardwalk into the Atlantic Ocean.

There was elegance in the salt air. Baskets of gladiola decorated the awninged clubhouse for the annual Moonlight White Flannel Dance. Musicians in sailor suits entertained guests, who carved elaborate cakes provided by the Traymore Hotel and strolled midway down the pier to a stand for hot dogs and ice cream.

There was also, as expected, plenty of fishing at The Anglers Club—

one season, recorded landings exceeded ten thousand. Membership climbed past two hundred by 1933 and stayed at that level for a decade, as the clubhouse added a locker room and ladies' lounge. Then nature turned hostile.

The ferocious hurricane in September 1944 obliterated the pier (as it did the Margate stretch of the boardwalk) and severely damaged the clubhouse. Club president Henry Asam, a Philadelphia wallpaper executive, spearheaded the effort to rebuild "for the glory of the sport," as he was fond of saying. The membership responded by buying non-interest-bearing bonds (eventually repaid in full) to bankroll the project, and a new pier—one hundred feet longer than its predecessor—rose in 1945. The entrance shifted a few paces to its present site at the foot of Exeter Avenue; a simpler structure replaced the latticed archway. A shade less glorious than before, The Anglers Club was nonetheless back in business.

Fishing remained fruitful through the 1950s, as the future teenage member made his inaugural appearance on deck in short pants. Soon, however, Anglers Club vets began to complain that encroaching "Russian trawlers" were reducing the stocks—it was indeed the time of the Cold War. Wagering became as popular as fishing, as poker and clouds of cigar smoke held sway in the men's club room. Five illegal slot machines took up residence in the clubhouse, and the youth's grandmother showed an even better touch with the one-armed bandits than with her fishing pole.

Annual dinner dances at the Linwood Country Club perpetuated one tradition, but another was lost when founder Shaner died in 1965, after having served as the club's secretary since its inception. The next season, the extraordinary mentor Frank Young died, and on Memorial Day, the club president tossed roses into the oncoming tide.

The expansive, paneled clubhouse withstood an October 1988 fire of unknown origin that destroyed the front tee and forty feet of walkway. Again, the faithful raised money and produced, by spring 1991, the third incarnation of The Anglers Club. The ranks thinned during the hiatus, and time brought additional change: women now fished out front and became full-fledged members. A security gate divided the front tee, its shed, and its lineup of fishing rods from the rest of the pier. Kitchen facilities transformed the old TV room where broadcasts of New York Yankee games once stirred summer evenings. The slot machines were long gone.

But much remained as it was. The blackboard still displayed chalked bulletins of significant catches. Water continued to splash in the little basin where scales and stink were routinely removed from lathered hands. The locker room received a new coat of paint, but a visitor could still close his eyes and see some of the guys take a nip and lock up the evidence for safekeeping. Interclub contests continued to highlight the fishing season, and the Memorial Day and Labor Day buffets were as festive as ever. The kingfish remained king, blues ran in the fall, and some fish still grabbed the bait even when an angler set his rod down and put the reel on automatic; such oblivious fish were "committing suicide," members used to say.

Some things had improved. The bait-and-tackle shop had expanded, enabling members to fully equip themselves right on the premises. And for the women, a bonus: a color-coordinated, softly lit restroom worthy of any casino.

Outside, waves crashed on the beach's jagged rock pile, whose moss veneer was greener than remembered. The ocean's familiar din invigorated as ever, foam rushing over the hard sand below the pier. Sea gulls faced uptown, their feathers smoothed by a stiff southerly wind. Perched on the parallel railings like sentries, they guarded the footsteps of ghosts and new generations.

Skee-Ball

The monitors stood like palace guards, a broad stripe running the length of each pair of creased trousers. At one alley, a fat man wearing galluses hunched over the mahogany, rubbed his hands, and toed the floorboards as if he were ready to break into a tap dance. Next to him, a man in a vested suit licked his lips and squinted at the target. One spot over, a woman tugged at her flowing white dress and bent her knees. And so on down the line—all twenty-one lanes were occupied by players with eyes fixed straight ahead, while other contestants sat and smoked and awaited their turn. Light fixtures suspended from the ceiling by long metal rods illuminated the crowd and a rather ingenuous admission printed high on the wall: "Our task is to make this business more profitable by making it more pleasant."

The business at hand was the first National Skee-Ball Tournament, as 122 competitors from across the United States and Canada gathered in Atlantic City to demonstrate their skill. It was late September 1932, and the newspapers were busy with stories about Babe Ruth and the World Series, a presidential candidate named Franklin Delano Roosevelt, and economic hard times that were worsening daily.

But while the Depression had gripped the country, spirits stayed high at the seashore. Million Dollar Pier was hosting dance marathons, and Will Rogers and Laurel and Hardy were cavorting on local movie screens, as arcade enthusiasts (seating for 500 spectators) watched the weekend Skee-Ball tourney at the "stadium" at Florida Avenue and the boardwalk. One R. K. Stong, of East Greenville, Pennsylvania, captured the top prize of $1,000 after tallying 5,240 points in 21 games—one game on each alley. Skee-Ball had rolled into the national spotlight.

The game already resided in the popular imagination. In 1909, recent Princeton University graduate Jonathan Dickinson Este fashioned wood from his father's Philadelphia lumberyard into a game he called Box Ball. Coney Island impresario Maurice A. Piesen rechristened the bowlinglike game Skee-Ball and marketed it to the amusement industry during the World War I years. Piesen's National Skee-Ball Company produced machines that were thirty-six feet long and crafted of cypress and birch. When the alley length was reduced to fourteen feet several years later, the game expanded its appeal beyond the strong-armed and the eagle-eyed. Women, children, and grandparents now anted up their nickels for a game of nine balls, each rolled toward a sloping targetboard. Separate men's and women's scoring rules were the norm, and mechanical counters displayed point totals that corresponded to utilitarian prizes such as lamps, vases, dinner plates, and other housewares. Skee-Ball migrated to Chicago, Omaha, and points west, and appeared under the name Skee Roll at the 1939 World's Fair in New York. Portable units turned profits at carnivals and on roving

Skee-Ball is the no-frills, venerable arcade game that is a staple of the seashore.
PHOTOGRAPH BY ELIZABETH WILK

amusement trailers, bringing the game into neighborhoods beyond the big cities.

As Skee-Ball spanned generations, ownership changed hands. In 1935, the Rudolph Wurlitzer Company—known worldwide for its pianos and organs—acquired the rights from Piesen, who retained a royalty agreement. A decade later, the Philadelphia Toboggan Company, whose product line included carousel horses prized today as collectibles, purchased the Skee-Ball patent and trademark from Wurlitzer. Refinements, such as the automatic ticket dispenser (tickets were redeemable for goodies or additional rounds of play), eventually improved the bottom line, but the game itself remained uncomplicated and accessible.

Modern technology neither buried nor disfigured Skee-Ball. Electronic controls were introduced in the mid-1970s, and the ball-release lever and mechanical tote board yielded to sensors and digital computers. Flashing lights and sound effects joined the mix, but still, the game was the thing. Amusement industry polls reflected Skee-Ball's continued popularity, as its movement and strategy appealed to both the muscular and the cerebral.

There has always been something beguiling about Skee-Ball's simplicity. You cradle a brownish, grapefruit-size ball of compressed wood, crouch in concentration, swing your arm like a pendulum, and let fly. The ball rolls down the alley until it scoots under a wire mesh and hops off a hump toward a series of holes that slant away from the screen at about a forty-five-degree angle. The higher the hole, the greater the point value; indeed, the force behind your toss should be a function of whether you are gunning for the fifty-point hole at the top (newer machines have added hundred-point holes) or taking the more conservative route of aiming lower for targets of lesser point values. Miss the fifty and your ball will most likely ricochet off the ledge that surrounds the hole and then spiral to the bottom, where your total score increases by only ten points. The sensation is akin to throwing a gutter ball in bowling.

With the ball negotiating the pivotal hump and accelerating upward toward target holes bounded by circular pathways, Skee-Ball resembles a kind of reverse ski slalom. It is easy to play, yet difficult to master, and that combination has helped make it a staple at the seashore.

When the electronic "brains" arrived more than twenty-five years ago, a design change shortened the Skee-Ball runway to thirteen feet, and even shorter lengths for smaller patrons became popular in family entertainment centers. In the 1980s, innovations included a four-player game, to encourage group competition, and electronic components that enabled arcade operators to reprogram game settings on location. By this time, Skee-Ball Inc. was split from its parent, Philadelphia Toboggan, and became a separate company with production facilities in Chalfont, Pennsylvania (in Bucks County just north of Philadelphia). As Skee-Ball machines rolled into Europe and Asia, their numbers grew to about eighty thousand, 25 percent of them less than a decade old.

At the Chalfont plant, sheets of plywood were stacked and then shaped into the alleys, sleeves, shelves, and cabinets of a new generation of Skee-Ball "Classic" machines and the jazzy newcomer "Lightning." Dramatic colors and graphics, fluorescent lights, dot matrix displays, interactive messages, and the rumble of thunder gave Lightning a contemporary profile, but the dynamics of play remained the same as those outlined by Este in 1909. On the production floor, Skee-Ball workers—sanders, painters, electricians—assembled new machines ticketed for locations from Tokyo to Wildwood.

This anchor game for many arcades and family fun centers remained nine rolls per game, though the cost jumped to a whopping quarter or more. In a high-tech world, Skee-Ball was holding its niche. And in an industry where some games and operators were deemed less pure than the driven snow, Skee-Ball seemed beyond reproach, with none of the come-on associated with amusement contests dominated by human operators (as in "step right up and win a prize"). Though its optional features now included a progressive jackpot linking as many as a dozen alleys, the game had not been infiltrated by high rollers. "While it is gambling in a sense, I cannot recall a single complaint on Skee-Ball," said one New Jersey state official.

With no rap sheet, a strong tradition, and a global marketplace, Skee-Ball was poised to continue its winning ways. Though the company no longer made mechanical replacement parts, some of the vintage machines were still in action at arcades in Coney Island, New York; Atlantic City and Ocean City, New Jersey; and some Maryland beach resorts. In most of these areas, the passing scene had changed radically during the past century, but boardwalks were still made of wood. So, too, Skee-Ball machines, and people continued to knock on both.

Ocean City Music Pier

Morning cuts through the curtains and drenches the room, etching jagged shafts of sunlight on the parquet floor. The young woman from Philadelphia sits at a writing desk and presses her feelings onto a postcard.

Furtively, she glances at two elderly ladies chatting on a nearby couch, then looks beyond the expansive arched windows to the sea, now tranquil and glinting under the high summer sky. The limpid melodies from the previous evening's concert still spin in her head, as she sways dreamily before returning to the task at hand.

> Dearest Billy,
>
> If separation is the true test of one's feelings, then I can honestly say what's in my heart. I wish you could be here with me.
>
> We are staying at the Flanders—a beautiful hotel by the beach.

Last night we went to a magnificent musical concert. The weather has been great—I think I'll go to the beach this afternoon. (Are you jealous yet?) Everything's wonderful with one exception: You are not here.

> Miss ya & love ya
>
> Gwen

Below, on the beach, a group of musicians plays softball, a folded towel designating home plate in the shadow of one of the many concrete pilings supporting the Ocean City Music Pier. The guitarist, who strummed on Rudy Vallee's radio show, cocks his bat. Planted in an outfield of wet sand is the violinist whose weepy refrains once accompanied the histrionics of silent-screen stars. Other members of the city's twenty-five-piece orchestra toss quoits and trade quips in the hot sun.

A boy hawks newspapers on the boardwalk by the Moorlyn Theater, where the marquee promises Henry Fonda in *Young Mr. Lincoln* and Jack Benny in *Man About Town*. From the Music Pier's second-floor library, the maestro watches the Fourth of July crowd swell. He turns away, mounts a stepladder, and plucks off the lofty shelves a waltz by Strauss and—fitting the occasion—a march by Sousa. Perusing the score, he simulates the familiar tempo, each puff of his lips a tuba blast.

Her pleated skirt flaring above black-and-white saddle shoes, seventeen-year-old Gwendolyn Martin walks out of the Music Pier solarium and onto the adjacent loggia. The ocean breezes swirl about the arches, as she looks southward and eyes a phalanx of exercisers—her parents among them—doing synchronized jumping jacks on the Twelfth Street beach. Nearby, rider and horse canter at the shoreline; this despite the city's recent ban on such forays.

Gwen steps past the outdoor pavilion benches, and swings around to the Music Pier's main entrance. She stops to read her words one last time. Inside, a post office summertime substation will send her postcard on its way.

By 1939, the Ocean City Music Pier was already a landmark. A decade earlier, it had displaced the white-frame Music Pavilion, which also led a second life as the city's convention hall on the Sixth Street boardwalk. The new structure at Moorlyn Terrace was built of sturdier stuff:

Booming orchestral and vocal sounds mingle with the roaring surf at the Ocean City Music Pier.
PHOTOGRAPH COURTESY OF THE *COURIER-POST*

concrete beams and columns, stuccoed exterior walls, a tiled roof, wrought-iron guardrails.

On July 4, 1929, hundreds of straw hats bobbed before a makeshift platform smothered with flags and bunting, as the town fathers dedicated the Music Pier and the new boardwalk that had risen from the ashes of the ravaging 1927 fire. The new pier was the crown jewel in Ocean City's revival.

The Spanish-style edifice, built at a cost of $248,000, quickly became the city's appointed spot for rendezvous and ceremony. But the real spirit of the place was nurtured by something other than image and architecture. Music counted more than mortar; the auditorium's orchestral and vocal performances seemed as natural as the Atlantic Ocean.

The music came from the masters: powerful arias by Puccini and Verdi and Bizet, the sweeping melodies of Tchaikovsky, the precision of Ravel, the magic of Mozart. Rousing scores by Gilbert and Sullivan never failed to delight. Broadway show-stoppers were preceded by the lilting operettas of Victor Herbert and Sigmund Romberg, with soloists like soprano Jeannette Stokes and baritone Tom Perkins delivering "Rose Marie" and "Donkey Serenade" and other romantic favorites that stirred all ages. A graduate of the Curtis Institute of Music, Perkins also served as emcee during his four decades at center stage, and he had a personality to match his pipes. His assortment of Irish ditties lightened many an evening of otherwise serious music.

Another classically trained musician synonymous with the Music Pier's history was Frank Ruggieri, who came aboard during the inaugural season. He played his bassoon for the then twelve-piece band, earning thirty dollars a week for the ten-week summer session of free nightly concerts. When local violinist J. Fred Manne took the helm in 1933, Ruggieri urged his new boss to expand both the orchestra and its repertoire. Manne concurred and appointed Ruggieri orchestra manager, and the ambitious bassoonist recruited musicians and purchased a library of film music for only five hundred dollars from Philadelphia's Stanley Theater. Soon enough, the orchestra doubled in size, and symphonic overtures filled the concert hall.

The 1930s also brought show music and dressy crowds—the men in white shoes and matching flannel trousers, blue jackets and Panama hats; the women in long white gloves, "sweetheart" necklines, and knitted stoles. They sat on wooden chairs and hummed along with the tunes of Cole Porter and Irving Berlin. The forties introduced the works of Rodgers and Hammerstein, and majestic lyrics resonated from the proscenium.

During the war years, the Music Pier demonstrated its functional versatility by sporting a rooftop tower geared for sightings of enemy aircraft and U-boats. The tower served its purpose—the island escaped attack.

Musical tastes grew changeable in the mass markets, but quality remained the watchword at the Music Pier. The reservoir of sheet music and arrangements guaranteed a different program every night.

Successors to Manne would include longtime conductor Clarence Fuhrman and, starting in 1974, top Broadway and Big Band arranger John Warrington, who further popularized the musical mix and christened the orchestra "Ocean City Pops." When Warrington fell ill during a 1978 performance, stepping into the breach was first-time conductor Frank Ruggieri. He stayed on the podium for seven more seasons, presiding over the embodiment of his own vision.

By this time, nearly six decades of onrushing tides had taken their toll on the Music Pier. But the city moved quickly to restore its monument, and upgraded facilities signaled an expanded entertainment menu.

The music plays on.

Gwen Morris (née Martin) has missed few beats, though she is well past her seventieth birthday. For her, the music still leads, and a concert by the sea is the finest partner possible.

Best of all, the Music Pier is as it was. The yellowish stucco topped by terra-cotta, the inviting arches, the huge granite urns lined up like sentinels—everything is in place. Pigeons still snack on the roof, people still gaze at the ocean, and music—real music—still graces the boardwalk. All is nearly right with the world.

Gwen and her Billy did go their separate ways, but that was several lifetimes go. While she was finishing high school, he was training with Uncle Sam. Though he survived World War II, Billy became William, and life grew complicated.

Gwen was thinking of that not long ago when her fifteen-year-old granddaughter attended a Friday night teen dance at the Music Pier and was visibly attracted to a young man who moved with a certain swagger. "Don't misunderstand, he's basically a good boy," Gwen insisted. His haircut—at least on the sides—had reminded her of Billy's old pictures from boot camp.

She wanted to caution Kristen that love can be a flighty thing, even though love songs last forever.

The Cowtown Rodeo

The cowboy crunches the dusty trail, spurs jangling, eyes uncompromising, on his way to the arena to tame the wild things.

The objects of his concentration are the bucking broncos and careening steers of rodeo fame. But there is another restless critter fueling his intent: the cowboy's own untamed heart. Vestige of the frontier, rugged independence corralled for modern exhibition.

And so he steps toward the crucible, past the trucks and trailers parked under a broiling sun, past ponies lazily swishing their tails and munching on tall grass, toward the bluff where chicken wire is strung between wooden posts, and there waits a generous watering hole fit for an outlaw's rendezvous.

In the arena: the fury to come. Handlers settle rider and beast in the chute, and from that compressed, fenced-in, secure space emerges the dauntless duo: a ton of wild animal and the rip-roarin' rider tenuously tethered to a rigged rope and/or a pair of stirrups. For eight heaving seconds, he must stay atop the movable mountain, or kiss the unforgiving turf.

Cowtown Rodeo, in Pilesgrove Township near Woodstown, Salem County, has completed forty-six seasons and is one of only a few weekly rodeos in the United States. The setting is the expansive grounds of Cowtown Ranch, where horses, cows, and bulls (and pigs and sheep) are raised for rodeo or sale in livestock auctions.

Cowtown began as one of the first public cattle auctions in the country, gaveled into existence by Howard Harris in 1926 and a family operation ever since. Howard Jr. (known as Stoney) joined his father, expanded the concessions, and cut quite a figure on horseback, riding up and down the midway. It was on the watch of Howard Harris III, Idaho University's "All-Around Intercollegiate Cowboy of the Year" in 1954, that the rodeo kicked into high gear, bursting through the gates on Saturday nights and branding ABC for a national television spot.

In the late seventies, Grant Harris purchased the rodeo from his father, moving Cowtown operations to a fourth generation.

The quintessentially American sport of rodeo grew out of the informal celebrations held by nineteenth-century cowboys after they had rounded up (*rodeo* is the Spanish word for round-up, its usage reflecting the Mexican influence in the American Southwest) their cattle and driven them to market. Ambitious cowpokes were not reluctant to bet their wages on competitions displaying their roughhewn working skills.

While the National Rodeo Finals have received Las Vegas hoedowns and ESPN broadcasts, the sport's lifeblood courses through small towns and rural countryside, through frontier outposts and sprawling ranches in big-sky stretches like Cheyenne, Calgary, Salinas, . . . and New Jersey.

Cowtown's Saturday night shows run from Memorial Day weekend to late September, and contestants must be members of the Professional Rodeo Cowboys Association, about seventeen thousand strong.

The bronco won this round, but at the Cowtown Rodeo, the cowboys always bounce back.
PHOTOGRAPH COURTESY OF THE *COURIER-POST*

While others are still donning their duds in the parking lot, the cowboy makes his way into the arena, where the P.A. announcer shouts tidings. When the cavalcade unfolds, riders trot out astride their horses followed by the Cowtown mares and their young—the next generation of equine stars.

The field is cleared, the audience leans forward, and out of a chute comes the next odd couple, a bareback rider aboard a bronc with an attitude. Bareback riding is one of three "roughstock" events requiring that the rider stay mounted for at least eight seconds. Contestants may place only one hand on animal and equipment, the free hand swiping at air.

The judges award points for style and proficiency . . . and survival.

Some of the riders are dumped ingloriously on their britches. But they will ride another day.

On to bull riding, an interlock of courageous cowboy and big bad bull. Then the choreography of calf roping, with the lariat floating toward its mark, the calf stopped in its traces, the roper dismounting promptly, his—or her—horse moving backward in mincing steps to keep the rope taut. The capper is the expert tying of any three of the calf's legs, a crowd-pleasing flourish. The calf is a tough creature, rodeo pros say, and treatment humane.

Steer wrestling and barrel racing are yet to come in the gathering twilight before the athletes (four- and two-legged) call it a night, and the angular, solitary cowboy makes his way out of the arena, through the parking lot, and back onto the trail that tracks the horizon. A little shut-eye before the next sunrise.

ROOM & BOARD ✦

The Shelburne

The baby came at midnight in a shack that slept seven behind the hotel. Daniel Reynolds was not present when his son, Joshua, first sampled Atlantic City nightlife; he was preparing a special meal in the hotel kitchen. The 1890s were not gay for everyone.

Meanwhile, his immense appetite stoked by the boardwalk's bright lights, railroad magnate James Buchanan "Diamond Jim" Brady waded into the dining room. Rocks sparkled on his fingers and vest, and his hair was slick and parted down the middle, thanks to an afternoon session at the tonsorial parlor. On his arm, a stately woman in silk evening dress swept into the room. A tilted, plumed hat shaded her limpid blue eyes, and pearls dripped to her corseted waist. For Lillian Russell, the diva-siren of her day, each entrance was a command performance.

If their relationship was platonic, they shared a love affair with the knife and fork. Deviled crabs garnished a mountainous salad, vats of oysters and tureens of turtle soup disappeared, lamb chops went like crackers—all chased by a box of chocolates. Even then, the Hotel Shelburne was known for its epicurean delights.

Two decades later, Brady's death would mark the end of an era. After a lifetime of high living, the gastronomic Gargantua had a busted stomach. He had built a fortune in the railroad and steel industries, and a reputation as a bon vivant nonpareil, a patron of the theater, and a soft touch. Ultimately, the spotlight proved to be a harsh taskmaster for Diamond Jim. On New Year's Day in 1917, he left his native Gotham one last time for the seashore, commandeered a sumptuous suite at the Shelburne, and wrapped his declining bulk in a steamer chair on

The regal Shelburne, with its angular profile and towering steeple,
seemed like a building poised to take a bow.

PHOTOGRAPH COURTESY COLLECTION OF VICKI GOLD LEVI

the glass-enclosed porch. Doctors and nurses doted, but the string had been played.

On April 12, the erstwhile titan of the rails gripped his diamond-studded cane and settled into a rolling chair for his customary ride. A young Josh Reynolds pushed the big man along the boards that day; Brady waved at the sea of faces and chatted with the familiar ones. The next day he was gone.

The United States had just entered World War I. The age of indulgence was over.

The Hotel Shelburne was born in stricter times. Elisha Roberts, scion of a Philadelphia Quaker family who had accompanied William Penn to this rugged new land, built the original wooden hotel in 1869. Featuring a deep veranda, the frame structure overlooked a boardwalk flush with the beach. Among other noted guests, Civil War hero Ulysses S. Grant paid a visit.

A footnote to an earlier upheaval had given his name to the hotel. William Petty-Fitzmaurice had been First Marquess of Lansdowne and Second Earl of Shelburne in title-mad Britannia. Lord Shelburne also had been prime minister late in the American Revolution and favored revoking the colonies' taxes. Legend has it that King George III showed him the gate, but in truth, Shelburne's premature exit from government was a case of political infighting with powerful statesman William Pitt.

Regardless, his was a noble name for a noble hotel, and the famous Shelburne crest—winged horses flanking crossed swords—conjured up the bygone days of heraldry. On hotel stationery and, later, sculpted on an outside wall, the emblem's Latin phrase "Virtute non Verbis" (Deeds, not Words) promised a level of quality that flashing lights can't quite convey.

In 1877, the Shelburne threw its doors open to winter guests. A quarter century later, when fastidious hotelier Jacob Weikel purchased the property from Roberts, a room fetched three to five dollars a day, and the hotel became a rendezvous for show business luminaries. Dinner parties dazzled with Diamond Jim, his consort Miss Russell, and

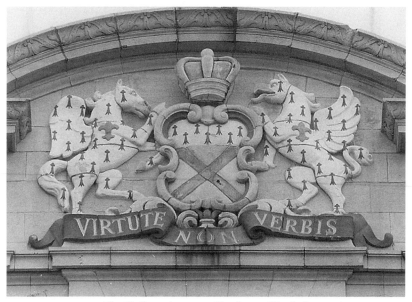

The Shelburne's motto: "Deeds, not Words."
PHOTOGRAPH COURTESY OF THE *COURIER-POST*

another beauteous Lil: British enchantress Lillie Langtry. Composer Victor Herbert was a frequent guest when he was in town to mount his popular operettas at the Apollo and Globe theaters. The likes of Ethel Barrymore, Al Jolson, and Irving Berlin often signed the register after viewing, or giving, a performance at the colorful Hippodrome on nearby Million Dollar Pier.

One day, as Broadway giant George M. Cohan regaled visitors in his room facing the ocean, a certain bellhop was hauling luggage in the lobby like a one-man freight company. Upstairs, the magnetic Cohan previewed his newest tune; the instant anthem was a rousing warning to the Hun. "Over there! Over there . . . the Yanks are comin'," he shouted, and indeed, soon after, the dogged bellhop—now Private J. Reynolds—was dodging gunfire in the forests of France.

The Stars and Stripes prevailed and, in July of 1927, the Shelburne hosted a gala breakfast to kick off storied bandleader John Philip Sousa's final engagement at the Steel Pier just up the boardwalk. By this time, Weikel had built an all-brick edifice in front of the vintage hotel, expanding capacity from 80 to 325 rooms plus a penthouse. This structure became the familiar, courtly Shelburne of the Atlantic City skyline: two-tiered, the taller rear crowned by a pointed steeple and spire.

Sculpted swans perched at the base of the steeple just above a cornice of terra-cotta urns. Across Michigan Avenue was the historic Dennis, which still stands, enveloped into Bally's Park Place casino-hotel. The Shelburne, however, owned the corner. Its classic trim, architectural richness, and distinctive shape gave it a regal warmth. It was a building poised to take a bow.

Inside, the gracious reputation was fixed by visual splendor, French cuisine, and continental service. The fourteenth-floor (there was no thirteenth) penthouse had gold fixtures in its seven bedrooms and baths, and a living room that ran the width of the building. Just below, an expansive outdoor balcony offered all guests a commanding view of the ocean. At ground level, carved mahogany burnished the lobby, where the checkered floor was adorned with Oriental rugs. A grand staircase rose from the entrance on Michigan Avenue. The formal dining room wore the elegance of white-glove service and gauzy Irish linen, while tuxedoed waiters deftly arranged china and silver aside table lamps. On the walls, murals captured impressionistic beach scenes on sixty feet of canvas, and through the plate-glass windows, a waterfall played among the flowers.

By the end of World War II, impresario Frank Gravatt, who had made the Steel Pier a showplace, owned the Shelburne, and his eccentric ways pushed the hotel to new heights. Known to prowl the hallways before sunrise, he would unscrew light bulbs and sprinkle talcum powder on the carpet as he made his rounds. When general manager Joseph Hitzel arrived, he'd spot the flaws and redouble his efforts. Shelburne operations were studied in hotel management courses, and the graceful building became a year-round address for the retired rich.

The heyday, though, was winding down. Max Malamut, who owned several other Atlantic City hotels, acquired the property in 1950 and added a ballroom behind the original wooden structure. The complex reached Pacific Avenue when the Empress Motel debuted in the mid-fifties, and the new Maple Leaf Skating Rink courted Canadian tourists. The subsequent motel boom clashed with the fading grandeur of the boardwalk hotels, and the city sagged as property values sank. Only the ocean was immutable, nature's effortless mockery of our mortal empire ashore.

But the empire builders were readying a comeback destined to give the skyline a new signature.

Santa, his reindeer, and his sleigh were still fronting the garlanded pillars of the Shelburne entrance on January 2, 1969, when Atlantic City embraced the future. Local business and political leaders convened in the hotel's Diamond Jim Brady Room, where the air was thick with the scent of hydrangeas and money. As the brain trust plotted a fundraising strategy to draw the casino industry to the Shore, the old order began to slip away.

Within eight years, the gambling referendum passed, and most of the boardwalk hotels numbered their days. The Malamuts tried to give the Shelburne a new incarnation, but could never quite strike a deal. Debts mounted and the hotel fell into disrepair. By the early seventies, health and fire inspectors were threatening a shutdown. Soon, the doors closed for the winter season. In 1978, all but the first two floors were off-limits; late that year, the building closed for good.

It was the last of the grand old hotels to fall. The crane and wrecking ball made their appearance in late July 1984, as police dispersed a group of homeless who had found shelter behind the boarded, first-floor windows.

The deathwatch lingered. Halfway through the seven-week demolition, as the iron ball swung and earthmovers attacked the rubble, the faithful gathered on the boardwalk to see the steeple topple to earth. As he did most days, an old man walked from his apartment on Missouri Avenue to join the curious and the mournful. As he looked through the hole in the thin wall of wood that separated the spectators from the work site, Joshua Reynolds, now eighty-seven and growing frail, knew all too well the town's journey from restricted colored quarters to casino high rollers. He owed this hotel nothing; he had sweated at the Shelburne while others luxuriated.

But it was a piece of him, and as the pieces crumbled, it was almost too painful to watch.

The Marlborough-Blenheim Hotel

Tea time begins at four o'clock sharp with the tinkling of bells and the promise of elegance. Down a sun-soaked corridor stroll elderly couples, nattily dressed and eager to answer the summons. A young girl clings to her grandmother, who in turn locks arms with her husband as they pass the music room layed with Oriental rugs and enter a lobby of Chippendale-style furniture and marble fireplaces. In the dining room, where the chandelier floats in glittering orbit and soft lights rim the base of the vaulted ceiling, suited waiters and crisp tablecloths form a sea of white. The tea stokes the guests, and a warm buzz fills the room.

Outside the hotel, the socializing is less measured. Bloomers and high spirits rule the beach, and dramatic shapes rise from the sand as if sculpted by the tide. The broad, oceanward face of the building is host to a thousand ornamental creatures, and a terra-cotta roof is perched just below the sky. Back inside, sitting with her ankles crossed and her white shoes dangling several inches above the thick carpet, the little girl gathers in her mind's eye the sea creatures and the sand sculpture and all the wondrous images of her castle-by-the-sea. Somehow, she feels they will last forever.

They were sisters who looked nothing alike. With its hooded beveled windows, a flared roof like a giant top hat, and front porches drinking ocean breezes, the Marlborough Hotel epitomized early nineteenth-century seashore grace. Its stone base yielded to a reddish wood frame, and other hues shifted in the sunlight like chameleons. Squat, brick posts anchored ornamental iron fencing that bordered manicured lawns.

Just steps away was another world: the Blenheim, a sultan's palace, testament to concrete and Moorish architecture. Cream-colored and imperial, it was a mélange of sharp edges, sloping curves, angled windows, and towering lookouts. Two monoliths—like robotic arms in upright position—fronted a great golden dome flanked by a pair of open-air cupolas, and an awninged pavilion topped three circular solariums and boardwalk shops touting imported goods. This was the original Taj Mahal on the Atlantic City skyline.

The dissimilar hotels were joined by an enclosed bridge spanning Ohio Avenue, and for seventy-two years the Marlborough-Blenheim was a destination for generations of well-heeled families, "the newly-wed and the nearly dead."

First came the Marlborough in 1902, when builder Josiah White III purchased land adjacent to Park Place and tapped Philadelphia architect William I. Price to design a structure named after the home of England's Prince of Wales. Among the hostelry's innovations was a system that circulated ice water to every room. White was content with his single site, but fortunately for the history of resort architecture, the Children's Seashore House next door soon moved downbeach to Chelsea and was replaced by an amusement park. By 1905, Marlborough patrons had grown weary of the roller coaster's roar; White and Sons bought the parcel, dismantled the rides, and—on a roll of their own—asked Price for what would become his masterwork. That was to be the Blenheim.

The blueprint was inspired and the materials borrowed from genius. Concrete for the hotel was purchased from the Edison Portland Cement Company founded by Thomas Alva Edison in 1899, and the Wizard himself came to town to supervise the pouring. As a wooden platform groaned under sacks of cement, hardhats surveyed the steel beams and shipments of tile earmarked for the Marlborough House Annex, a $670,000 project estimated to surpass a million dollars with furnishings. Crews dug an eighty-five-foot-deep artesian well guaranteed to provide the "finest crystal-clear water available." Natural elements and human processes coalesced, and the edifice was completed the following year.

In its splendor and complexity, it seemed a mirage. The generic Annex was renamed to honor the famous 1704 battle in Germany in which the first Duke of Marlborough (ancestor of Winston Churchill) led English-Austrian forces to victory over France's Louis XIV, a milestone also commemorated in the name of the family's great palace near

*A crosswalk tethered the genteel Marlborough (right) to the imperial
Blenheim, forming one hotel.*
PHOTOGRAPH COURTESY OF THE *COURIER-POST*

Oxford. Tethered to the Marlborough, the Blenheim was indeed royalty with a handmaiden.

The first completely fireproof hotel in Atlantic City and the first
to equip every room with a private bath, the Blenheim was known for
its conservative, stately traditions as well as its accoutrements. The
afternoon-tea ritual reportedly inspired lyricist Irving Caesar to pen
the words to the song "Tea for Two" one day in 1925 in the lobby. For
many years, the hotel's resident chamber-music trio played classical
selections daily for the dinner crowd. The beachfront sundeck was the
chosen spot for suitable doses of warmth and private conversation.

Quakers by faith, the White family insisted on taste and civility.
That perspective eventually clashed with the changing face of the boardwalk. And as the pace of society quickened, the underpinnings of the
grand hotels grew unsteady. By the 1970s, the Marlborough-Blenheim
was decidedly out of step.

After voters approved gambling for Atlantic City, investors sought to preserve at least the majestic Blenheim and convert it to a casino-hotel. But modernization was deemed too costly and, finally, unsafe.

Still, the Blenheim had achieved landmark status on both state and national historic registers, and an enthusiastic band of citizens known as Friends of the Marlborough-Blenheim Hotel lobbied to keep it alive. Meanwhile, the new owner, Chicago's Bally Manufacturing Company, prepared to blast away.

Change had its way. The wood-frame Marlborough went first in October 1978, the wrecking ball splintering its now shabby gentility into a monstrous pile of pickup sticks. A month later, demolition experts rigged the Blenheim for its demise. A thousand spectators stood on nearby balconies and rooftops, and behind police barricades blocks away, as 325 pounds of strategically placed dynamite brought down the eight-story wing that reached toward Pacific Avenue.

But there was life yet in the Blenheim—the palatial rotunda had been severed beforehand from the doomed section and remained standing, its dome winking through the billowing smoke. For the next several weeks, a last-ditch battle ensued: the Friends railed; the state listened but signed the death warrant.

On January 4, 1979, a second surge finished the job. Scrolls and statuary tumbled to earth. The dome crumpled and disappeared. The twin monoliths fell like giant redwoods, one of them bobbing in air for a frozen moment—a final twitch of protest—before toppling.

A vestige of the departed hotel was rescued and mounted in a corner of the courtyard at Bally's Park Place. The weathered three faces of Neptune once watched the coastline from the heights of the Marlborough-Blenheim. Now, the lime-green gargoyle sat on a black pedestal, an inscription at the base to educate passersby. Looming across the lawn: the former Dennis Hotel, a survivor that Bally's whitewashed, gutted, and refurbished as part of its accommodations.

An old woman reclines on a lounge chair, a light shawl wrapped about her to ward off the dampness. Much has changed in seven decades. Gone are the decorative lampposts that bathed strollers in the glow of five oversize bulbs. The tall windows of the boardwalk shops have shrunk and some are boarded up. People seem to move and talk and dress differently these days.

Still, this is her favorite spot in the world, and her memories are as finely etched as cut crystal. She comes here most every day to sip tea, relax, and remember. Today, however, is her last time. The president of the hotel—she knows the man personally—appears on the deck in the late afternoon. He cannot look the stragglers in the eye. "We're closing," he announces in a faraway voice, "the hotel is closing . . . I'm sorry."

With that, he marches away as a wizened attendant lowers and folds the flag for good, signals rich with regret that this is, after all, just a castle in the sand.

A Resort with a Historical View

Stern and dapper, their golf clubs propped like walking sticks, they stand on the sloping lawn as the photographer opens his shutter. Warren G. Harding wears knickers, knee socks, and a bow tie, his white hair topping dark bushy eyebrows and chiseled features—truly a Central Casting pick for president of the United States. Host Clarence H. Geist, a man of self-made wealth, has a face like a clenched fist. The stately, sweeping clubhouse looms behind them. Later that crystalline May afternoon in 1922, Harding would remark that his two days at Geist's Seaview Country Club have been the greatest he ever spent. But if the president's days are numbered (he will die in office the next year after a siege of scandal), Seaview has a long history yet to unfold.

One that is still being written. Bounded by bay waters and piney woodlands, the Absecon showpiece—now Seaview Marriott Resort—hosts the LPGA's ShopRite Classic Tournament each summer, as its famed Bay Course challenges the fastest growing event on the ladies' tour.

Golf is a sport accustomed to lush, dramatic settings, but Seaview's blend of the rustic and the elegant gives it a charm too often bulldozed away by the dictates of development. Think Churchill Downs burnishing the Kentucky Derby. Or Fenway Park, that backyard of a ballpark

Glamour golf: President Warren G. Harding (second from left), Seaview founder Clarence Geist (far left), New Jersey senator Joseph Frelinghuysen (third from left), and an unknown fourth complete a stylish quartet at Seaview Country Club, circa 1922.
PHOTOGRAPH COURTESY OF SEAVIEW MARRIOTT RESORT

where Boston Red Sox fans feel like they can just about slide into second base. Intimacy, compactness, and a natural beauty are the qualities that mark both the Bay Course and its partner across Route 9, Pines Course.

Carved out of the woods as a nine-hole course in 1929 (years after the debut of Bay Course) and expanded to 18 in the late 1950s, the Pines figured in the most notable of Seaview's early tournaments: the 1942 PGA Championship. Competition entailed match play (one-on-one, thirty-six holes a round, evenly divided between the two courses), and the tourney launched the legend of golfer Slammin' Sammy Snead. In white shirt and tie, pleated pants, and signature hat, Snead chipped in from sixty feet for a birdie on the thirty-fifth hole of the final round, besting Corporal Jim Turnesa, whose buddies from Fort Dix had crammed the gallery. It was Snead's first victory in a major tournament. He entered the navy the next day, but his sweet swing would soon return to the links.

By this time, Seaview was nearly three decades old and ownership had passed from late founder Geist to a group of local investors. Geist didn't need a group—he was an individualist. And something of an eccentric.

Born in 1874, the imperially minded Geist came to the seashore from LaPorte, Indiana, via Chicago, found a mentor in South Shore Gas Company officer Charles Dawes (Calvin Coolidge's future vice president), and began acquiring and consolidating regional gas companies. Aside from cash, his passion was golf. According to local lore (stories about Geist tend to fall into that realm), the utility king grew peeved one day while waiting—too long, he felt—to tee off at the Atlantic City Country Club, the course of choice for movers and shakers. Fellow member Maurice Risley, an Atlantic City realtor, suggested that Geist build his own club. Geist warmed to the idea, Risley fingered some scenic acreage just north of Absecon, and, in 1912, Seaview was built around a farmhouse that has long been the resort's brick-walled Grille, featuring publike ambience and first-class fare.

Geist may have been an impatient golfer at the Atlantic City Country Club (located on Shore Road in Northfield), but on his own turf, he proceeded at a leisurely pace, reportedly holding up following foursomes by swapping stories or playing a hand of poker with cronies in his limousine, which was poised to ferry them to the next hole. When he wasn't calling bluffs and stalking birdies, though, the well-heeled Geist catered largely to captains of industry and believed in amenities for them. Uniformed chauffeurs were on call to transport guests in limos with wood trim and running boards. (The garage where they resided now houses golf carts.) Vintage Seaview also offered horses, squash and tennis courts, a trap-shooting range, and the culinary creations of a French chef.

Today's facility, a Marriott property since 1984, retains the Old World, Gatsby-esque charm. The 670 acres haven't gone anywhere, nor has the four-story, seashore-white hotel whose 300 guest rooms recently received a four-million-dollar makeover. The main dining room, with its glittering chandelier and recessed ceiling, could double as a planetarium. Bay breezes waft through the carpeted lobby, where gracious furnishings evoke a tableau of white suits and chilled lemonade.

Outside, the sweeping circular driveway and porte-cochere announce Seaview's hold on yesteryear. The Atlantic City skyline shimmers in the distance, as seagulls glide and squawk above Reeds Bay and the brown marshes that stretch toward the golf course greenery. The fairways may be tranquil or capricious—many years ago, swirling bay zephyrs prompted the redoubtable Ben Hogan to label one of Bay Course's holes the toughest he had ever played.

The prevailing scent in the wind, however, is that of easy grace. Manicured lawns meld with rustic golf courses, and the stately hotel commands the slope. The gruff ways of Clarence Geist are gone, but not his vision. Time is more illusion than imperative.

If only Warren G. had kept playing and not returned to Washington.

Captain Starn's

This slice of 1950s seashore promised plentiful eye-candy and a full belly. While a line of hungry patrons snaked from the restaurant's canopied entrance onto the gravel parking lot, another crowd gathered at the midway to drop coins in the wishing well and watch sea lions cavort in watery pens, their cheerful barking guaranteed to raise a smile. A tiled lobster pool housed oblivious crustaceans ticketed for somebody's dinner plate. "Out of the water and into the pan," said the sign on the restaurant; perhaps the sea lions were happy because they knew they would avoid that steaming fate.

A different species crammed the docks, where fishing and excursion boats welcomed anglers and sightseers. The sinewy currents of Absecon Inlet shouldered the land, cutting a swath through the barrier islands, bringing tidings from the beach and ocean downstream. Crewcut kids hopped on speedboats and braced for the surge. Cameras clicked, motors revved.

Mates and captains readied their launches. One captain—the maker of the feast—grabbed the rail of a cruiser and leaned into the breeze. He sighted the drawbridge to Brigantine, low-slung on the horizon,

*The broad front of Capt. Starn's restaurant, complete with
canopied entrance and the Yacht Bar, in the early 1950s.*
PHOTOGRAPH BY FRED HESS, COURTESY COLLECTION OF BOB RUFFOLO

then turned toward his younger seafaring companions jockeying for
space on deck.

This was his creation. With one finger to the wind, and another on
the pulse of commerce, he had rescued this forgotten site and made it
a showplace.

Capt. Starn's Restaurant and Boating Center, a longtime inlet icon seaward of the junction of Atlantic City's Maine and Caspian avenues,
had quite a ride, rising in 1940 from the ruins of a nineteenth-century
recreational hub and braving brutal storms and fickle tastes before
succumbing to the changing face of the island. Much more than just an
eatery, it was a kind of circus by the sea, a seeming work-in-progress
continually reshaped by expansion and new attractions.

Captain Clarence Starn, who resembled Dwight D. Eisenhower,
and may have been just as tough an executive, possessed a seaman's
vision and a promoter's flair. As a young fisherman, he landed a monster shark in South Jersey waters in 1922 and displayed the creature in a
tent at ten cents a glimpse. Years later, it was the Big Top atmosphere
of Capt. Starn's Restaurant and Boating Center that hooked paying
customers. A quartet of porpoises soared and splashed until the cold

water did them in—enter the sea lions. Thrill rides, such as the diving seaplane, gave intrepid souls stomach-churning excitement.

"It was scary," said Don Nyce, a Starn's employee for three decades, recalling the plane. "When that reversible-pitch propeller hit the water, you were thrown backward."

Nyce's résumé at Starn's included the position of mate aboard the venerable sailboat *Olive*, a member of an impressive fleet that, as surely as the marine life (both performers and platters), gave the inlet complex its colorful personality. The roster evoked the sea, the heavens, and classy ladies: *Bonito, Fair Star, Malabar, Venus, Endeavor, Julia C.,* the double-deck *Lora Lee* which ferried sightseers to Beach Haven twice daily, and the sloop *Helena G. Starn* (named after the boss's wife) built by rival restaurateur Harry Hackney for Starn himself a dozen years before Capt. Starn's served its first customers. The glamour line of *Miss Atlantic City* speedboats attracted celebrities on seashore visits, while the various *Captain Starn* boats (six altogether, the last built after Starn's death) harvested the sea.

Starn's business reinvigorated what had been a rich boating tradition on this scenic shoreline. The railroad men were the first to grasp its potential. In 1876, the Camden and Atlantic Railroad—prime mover of the early Atlantic City—built a pier and two-story pavilion at the site to accommodate growing crowds shuttled from the main terminal to the inlet by horse-drawn rail cars. The deep and generally calm waters suited opportunistic boatmen, who tied down at the new wharf and provided transport for fishing and gaming parties. In 1883, these sometimes contentious captains organized the Atlantic City Yachtsmen's Association, which leased docking rights from the railroad and held sway here until disbanding in 1935.

By that time, the social scene had found new outlets downbeach, and severe storms had diminished the inlet structures, including Hyman's Hotel and its expansive dining hall. Don Riddle, whose family had considerable real estate holdings on the island, ran the diminished operation, but business was barely treading water. The Pennsylvania Railroad, now the landowner, wanted more bang for the clang.

What the Pennsy really wanted was to sell the land and its associated riparian rights. So executive J. O. Hackenberger approached Clarence Starn, then an enterprising sea captain who had shifted his

The sprawling complex that was Capt. Starn's.
IMAGE COURTESY OF TOM HULME

sailboat operation from the inlet to Steel Pier. The inlet was ripe for a renaissance, said the railroad veteran. Starn liked what he heard and closed the deal. Soon after, Hyman's was dismantled and its lumber used to help build Starn's new restaurant. The existing pavilion, reduced to a single story, became the dining room, and, on June 26, 1940, Capt. Starn's opened for business.

The comeback was just beginning. During the next two decades, Starn transformed the area. Captain Charles Swann, a fellow Steel Pier operative, brought his sailboats to the inlet. Old-timers resurfaced to secure berths at Starn's expanding docks, and as they died off, Starn acquired their boats. The restaurant grew like a tadpole, sprouting an elongated main dining room adjoining the original, an upstairs dining room called the Captain's Bridge, the outdoor Captain's Mess, the serpentine Over-the-Sea Bar, and the separate Yacht Bar fashioned from a small yacht owned by a local judge. Starn added a marine supply shop, a packing house to ready his fleet's harvest, and a fresh fish market for customers who liked to cook at home.

"He was even a better businessman than a boatman," said Tom Hulme, who served as a mate aboard the *Helena G.* and compiled pictorial scrapbooks chronicling the history of Capt. Starn's.

The entrepreneurial Starn was a taskmaster—waitresses uniformly wore sailor collars and ties, and pity the girl whose crease wilted, or who forgot to place a sprig of parsley on the plate. The restaurant eventually grew to more than seven hundred and fifty seats and served two thousand meals a day in summertime, when two-hundred-plus employees prepared and delivered fried clam fritters, baked stuffed flounder, double-deck lobster, and broiled Alaskan crab. The tables and chairs were square and wooden, the napkins and tablecloths white linen, the motif nautical, the water view at sunset something special.

For those more interested in angling than aesthetics, fishing dockmaster Al Kurtz—a onetime mayor of Absecon—detailed the day's catch on live radio reports from the packing house. Meanwhile, Starn's nephew and namesake, Clarence "Skeetz" Apel, helmed the sightseeing operation, as the familiar sloops and speedboats veered from inlet to ocean, cruising as far south as the President Hotel before returning.

"We ran a million people up and down the beachfront each year," said John Kurtz, Al's son and Tom Hulme's fellow mate on the *Helena G.* "That doesn't exist now."

The train doesn't stop here anymore. Aside the Starn lot, railroad car barns yielded to trolleys and buses and then vanished along with the adjacent ball fields and amusement rides of Inlet Park. At water's edge, the immutable rock pile that girded Capt. Starn's now fortifies only vacant, leveled land.

Clarence Starn died in 1969, and though his business survived him by a decade, it was a period of painful decline. Fresh air and simple pleasures were no longer at a premium. Vandalism and parking lot muggings wounded the site that had weathered the Hurricane of '44. Casino interests eyed the property, but a deal proved elusive. (Local redevelopment plans have earmarked the land for residential housing.) In the late 1980s, as Skeetz Apel still climbed sagging stairs to his office overlooking a few clam boats at the end of the dock, casino buses sat in the parking lot.

In 1992, the bulldozers showed up.

On a sun-gilded afternoon not long ago, a fisherman stood on the rocks just beyond Maine and Caspian, while a flock of pigeons huddled on the lot behind him. The boardwalk ramp that once ushered customers to Capt. Starn's doorstep now ended in emptiness, all splintered planks and rusted railings.

But at nearby Gardner's Basin, the deck was alive with memories and camaraderie. Don Nyce, Tom Hulme, John Kurtz, Skeetz Apel, and a hundred others gathered for a reunion of Capt. Starn's employees and friends. The sky was their pavilion. They pointed across the cove to Captain Starn's stately house and the mast of the moored *Helena G.* They remembered everything: the raw bar at the Captain's Mess, the Captain's table where Starn sat at the rear of the main dining room, the pooled lobsters drifting toward their doom, the parsley-on-the-plate, the sailor collars, people dancing on the wooden cutout in front of the bandstand.

And now, as music filled the salt air, the celebrants danced yet again. Nimble and unrestrained, they glided into another era.

Somewhere, a sea lion was applauding.

*"Pop" Lloyd had Hall-of-Fame baseball skills,
but it was his humanity that people prized above all.*
PHOTOGRAPH COURTESY JOHN HENRY "POP" LLOYD COMMITTEE

SPORTS

The Black Honus Wagner

Edging off first base, the runner is a figure of coiled menace. The infield baking in the Havana sun is *his* territory, and once more he will assert dominion. It is the law of the jungle, and this is the most fearsome Tiger of them all.

The shortstop stands perfectly still, long arms hanging at his sides. But the languid pose masks a competitor's fiery heart and a baseball savvy born of a hundred tumbledown ballparks. Beneath his stockings are cast-iron shin guards sturdy enough to deflect the most furious slide and sharpest spikes.

As the runner breaks and the shortstop glides toward the second-base bag, the pitch sails high and outside. The catcher's throw, though, is true, and before he can claim second base, the sliding runner collides with the shortstop's iron-girded leg. There will be no theft this day, because not even Tyrus Raymond Cobb can intimidate John Henry Lloyd.

Fast-forward from 1910 to the late 1930s, and Lloyd is tugging on the uniform of the Johnson Stars as he sits on a stool in Atlantic City's All Wars Memorial Building. He leads his young charges across the street to the New York Avenue Playground field where the Sunday after-noon crowd is already gathering. "Big Boy" Jones arrives with his megaphone, drops dramatically to one knee, and booms out the line-ups. The wooden grandstand comes alive.

Late in the game, the Stars' manager reaches for a bat in the corner of the dugout, oils it with an ancient rag, and steps to the plate. The first pitch is a nasty, inside breaking ball that the pinch-hitter can't handle—strike one. As if chastened, he bows his head, grabs a handful of earth, rubs his large hands together, and recocks the bat. The next offering is dead-on, and though he is past fifty now, Lloyd has the level, left-handed swing of eternal youth. The batted ball is a projectile that rattles off the corrugated tin fence in right field. Favoring a damaged knee, Lloyd limps into second base, chuckling all the way. There is an unmistakable joy in this man's work—especially when he has knocked in the winning run.

The "John Henry" of poetry and mythology was a "steel-drivin' man." Fittingly, John Henry "Pop" Lloyd—ever the father figure and the soul of decency—laid track so that others might ride. After a winter of barn-storming in Cuba and other points south, Ty Cobb could return to the Detroit Tigers and the Major Leagues. For Pop Lloyd, it was back to the spotty scheduling and negligible pay of the Negro Leagues. During his prime, he was dubbed "the Black Honus Wagner." In truth, many students of the game regarded the Pittsburgh Pirate immortal as the White Pop Lloyd. His plaque at the Hall of Fame identifies him as "the finest shortstop to play in Negro baseball," but Lloyd needed a deter-mined local lobbying effort to break into the Cooperstown pantheon.

By the time he made Atlantic City his hometown in 1919, Lloyd was already a diamond legend. Born in Palatka, Florida, he had come north to begin his professional career in 1906. Playing for clubs in Philadel-phia, Chicago, and New York, he distinguished himself as a rangy short-stop who cooled the hottest grounders and scooped outfield-bound shots out of the air as if he were playing jai alai. His bat knew nothing but line drives.

During exhibition games, Lloyd so impressed John McGraw that the pugnacious New York Giant manager tried to recruit the shortstop to join the likes of Christy Mathewson at the Polo Grounds. The bid was quashed by McGraw's fellow big league barons, who would allow baseball's segregation clock to tick for another three-and-a-half decades. Still, black clubs consistently held their own against "establishment" pennant winners and all-star teams during off-season series played in tropical climes. Lloyd and other black players, typically, waited on tables between games. For them, status was confined to the playing field.

When Atlantic City Mayor Harry Bacharach transplanted a band of ballplayers from Jacksonville, Florida (near Lloyd's birthplace), it was only a matter of time before Lloyd—a role model before the term was coined—would take charge as player-manager. Soon, the Eastern Colored League was formed, and heavy hitters such as the Washington Potomacs, the Baltimore Black Sox, and the Harrisburg Giants traveled to the seashore to meet the Atlantic City Bacharach Giants. Fans spilled out of trolleys at South Carolina and Caspian avenues and, often, entered Bacharach Ballpark by wriggling through outfield fences that had been raided for firewood during the winter.

One summer afternoon, a forty-year-old Pop Lloyd—called the "kid manager" by the press—laced his eleventh consecutive base hit, a feat unmatched outside the sandlots. Lloyd failed to hit safely in his next at-bat but finished the day by cracking three straight singles. It was July 4, 1924, and a select group of Atlantic City baseball fans roared for an American hero.

Lloyd left the Bacharachs, returned to New York, and made more history. A red cap himself, as a youth, he now helped organize a special game to benefit the union of Pullman porters. When his New York Lincoln Giants became the first black team to take the field at Yankee Stadium, he lingered in the dugout and discussed baseball with Babe Ruth.

Lloyd vowed to keep taking his cuts "until a left-hander strikes me out." When he reached the age of forty-eight, he retired from top-flight baseball, but played an astonishing ten more years with the Stars, a semipro team bankrolled successively by local political bosses Nucky Johnson and Hap Farley. The Stars eventually moved west—but just a few blocks—to a field at Indiana and Huron avenues. There, the even-tempered Lloyd groomed a new generation of athletes for life on and off the base paths, and there he stood before the microphones in the fall of 1949, as city officials dedicated the field to him. Trim and still springy in his suit and tie, Lloyd dabbed his forehead, then his eyes. The years of exclusion had retreated, and with them the opportunities. But for Lloyd, the city's simple acknowledgment was everything.

The elderly Lloyd became everybody's pop and a unique ambassador of good will. Young people flocked to him, warmed by his kindliness and entranced by his old baseball stories. Mature black athletes sought his counsel—racial obstacles were giving ground, but conflict abided, and who better to offer wisdom than Pop Lloyd, a first-class human being long consigned to a second-class role.

But the disparity between his place in the heart and his station in society was stark. This church leader, commissioner of the Westside Little League, and former titan of the playing field labored in a series of custodial jobs with City Hall, the post office, and the school district. Yet, there was something magical about the man that transcended normal yardsticks. Call it dignity, call it courage; it was a quality that frequently compelled Jim Usry, then principal of Indiana Avenue School, to spell the aging Lloyd and mow the school lawn himself. The future mayor of Atlantic City revered Lloyd. He was hardly alone.

It took a concerted educational campaign by Usry, Farley, and several local sports journalists to convince the Hall of Fame to open its portals to Lloyd in 1977, thirteen years after his death. His was not a household name.

The grass that once needed trimming on Indiana Avenue is covered by concrete now. Memories of old ball players dim in the sunburst of today's headlines. Certainly, we are all creatures of our time, and so it was with Pop Lloyd. Though not allowed to sit there, he helped set the table for future black professional baseball players. Jackie Robinson was the first to pull up a chair, followed by such greats as Willie Mays, Hank Aaron, and Ernie Banks (who was enshrined in the Hall the same day as was Lloyd), all the way to today's high-powered game of Barry Bonds and Ken Griffey Jr.

No telling what Lloyd would command in the current market. But his inscription in Cooperstown ("personified the best qualities of an athlete") is a much grander tribute than a shower of statistics or the fattest multiyear contract.

Indoor Bowling: Football Variety

It was four days before Christmas in 1963. Holiday cheer was in short supply as Liberty Bowl president Bud Dudley watched Mississippi State and North Carolina State battle in the fifth annual Liberty Bowl at Memorial Stadium. Temperatures in the low twenties combined with winds that reached seventeen miles per hour had frozen the wallets of most college football fans. Only 8,309 showed up to watch Mississippi State edge North Carolina, 16–12. Dudley had a bigger number on his mind: 93,691. That was how many seats were empty during the game at the cavernous stadium in South Philadelphia.

The first Liberty Bowl in 1959 had attracted thirty-six thousand fans, but attendance had declined each subsequent year. To save the Liberty Bowl, Dudley needed a venue immune to the weather. If it could capture the attention of the media, so much the better.

Dudley found the answer in Atlantic City's Convention Hall. Although the Liberty Bowl would reside there for just one season, it would be the first of three different bowl games played at Convention Hall over the next decade. By landing the Liberty Bowl, Atlantic City captured a slice of the football spotlight. Unknown to many sports fans, Convention Hall had a long association with football. The boardwalk facility, which opened in May 1929, had the distinction of hosting the first indoor college football game when Lafayette played Washington Jefferson in 1930. Similarly, the 1964 Liberty Bowl, pitting Utah against West Virginia, would be the first indoor bowl game in the history of college football.

Convention Hall was an architectural marvel among sporting arenas. Until the Astrodome opened in Houston in 1965, Convention Hall was the largest room without pillars in the United States. At 137 feet high, it was large enough to allow a helicopter to touch down inside the building.

When Utah and West Virginia squared off on December 19, 1964, the temperature was a chilly thirty-one degrees outside, a comfortable sixty degrees inside. "It was the only bowl game I ever promoted where a coach complained it was a bit too warm," Dudley quipped.

As *Philadelphia Evening Bulletin* sports columnist Sandy Grady observed, it was "a new kind of Liberty Bowl—no frostbite, no hip flasks, no icy ear lobes." Indoor football, dubbed "parlorball" by Grady, avoided the elements, including, in this case, the element of suspense, as Utah, led by future Pittsburgh Steelers star Roy Jefferson, trounced West Virginia, 32–6.

The game was a qualified success. Players and coaches for both teams praised the indoor field—real sod, not artificial turf, was used. Playing the game indoors allowed ABC television, which broadcast the game to a national audience, to try out unique camera angles. The network placed a camera thirteen floors about the ground to provide an aerial view of the plays unfolding.

Jack Gould, writing for the *New York Times*, was impressed by what he saw. "The perspective was little short of astonishing. The legendary seat on the fifty-yard line has lost its status as the best place to watch a game," he wrote.

Tickets sales, though, were a bit disappointing. Only 6,059 out of a possible 12,000 seats were sold at $10 dollars a seat. A capacity of 50 percent, however, still was markedly better than the minuscule 8 percent for the previous year at Philadelphia Stadium. Thanks to $95,000 in broadcast fees paid by ABC, Dudley garnered a $5,000 profit, which was donated to local charities. The Liberty Bowl, however, moved on in 1965 to Memphis, Tennessee, where it has been played ever since.

Atlantic City did not have to wait long to host another bowl game. The National Collegiate Athletic Association (NCAA) instituted a series of regional championship games for division II schools in 1964. From 1964 to 1967, the Eastern regional championship game was played in Orlando, Florida, and was known as the Tangerine Bowl. The game shifted to Atlantic City in 1968 was renamed the Boardwalk Bowl.

The first Boardwalk Bowl, on December 14, 1968, featured the University of Delaware's Blue Hens, with a 7–3 record, against the Big Indians of Pennsylvania's Indiana University, undefeated with nine victories.

"It was a great thrill for us to play there," recalled Tubby Raymond, the coach of Delaware. Both Raymond and his squad were playing in their first bowl game, but Raymond had some reservations about playing indoors, following a full season of football in the great outdoors. First, there was an end zone shortened by two yards because of the Miss America stage. Second, there were questions about the playing surface.

The 1969 Boardwalk Bowl, televised on ABC, pitted the University of Delaware against North Carolina Central University.
PHOTOGRAPH COURTESY COLLECTION OF VICKI GOLD LEVI

To prepare the hall for a football game, the ground crew put down a layer of burlap to help keep the sod and grass together. Theoretically, the optimal period for the sod to take root was two weeks, but the actual amount of growing time varied, depending on whether trade shows or other events were scheduled for the hall.

Raymond's fears about the field proved groundless. Delaware rallied in the game final's minute to defeat Indiana, 31–24. The game was a financial success, too, with 9,849 people attending despite television coverage throughout much of the East by ABC. A large contingent of Delaware fans attended the game, since the university was only a two-hour drive from Atlantic City. Coach Raymond remembered the weekend as a festive time, when many fans stayed in town overnight.

In four of the next five years, the Boardwalk Bowl had a distinctively blue cast, as Delaware's Blue Hens returned to play in 1969, 1970, 1971, and 1973. They defeated North Carolina Central in 1969, topped Morgan State in 1970, and crushed C. W. Post in 1971. Delaware's only loss came in 1973 when the team lost to Grambling, 17–8. Delaware turned down an invitation to play in 1972, and the University of Massachusetts defeated the University of California at Davis. Attendance averaged about ten thousand fans for the six games.

Atlantic City picked up its third bowl game in 1970, when the Knute Rockne Bowl, named for the legendary football coach of Notre Dame, was moved from Bridgeport, Connecticut, to Convention Hall. The Rockne Bowl, designed as a championship game for Eastern colleges in Division III, the smallest schools in the NCAA, was played there from 1970 to 1972. All three games were close contests. Montclair State edged Virginia's Hampden-Sydney, 7–6, in 1970. In 1971, Bridgeport defeated Hampden-Sydney, 17–12, then defended its title in 1972 by beating Slippery Rock, 27–22. Crowds were smaller than at the Boardwalk Bowl— in the two-to-three thousand range—but no less enthusiastic.

By 1974, changes in the NCAA's football playoff system spelled the end of the Boardwalk and Knute Rockne bowls. Still, college football continued to be played at Convention Hall. The last game played at the facility was on November 30, 1984, between Temple University, of Philadelphia, and the University of Toledo, ending—for now—a pigskin tradition that lasted more than half a century.

Goose Goslin

The 48,420 faithful jamming Detroit's Navin Field were ready to uncork delirium. Their Tigers had been frustrated four times in the World Series since the franchise's inception in 1901—just the previous autumn, Dizzy Dean and the St. Louis Cardinals had beaten them in the decisive seventh game. Now, at last, triumph was at hand.

Catcher-manager Mickey Cochrane edged off second base with two outs in the bottom of the ninth inning of a 3–3 game. Crowding the plate like an eagle hovering over its nesting young, the left-handed hitter ripped Chicago Cub hurler Larry French's first pitch foul into the lower right-field stands. French applied a little English to his second toss, but the Tiger batsman swung easy and floated one onto the center-field grass.

Cochrane broke immediately and tore around third base, a freight train roaring toward destiny. There was no play at home; the Tigers were king of the baseball jungle, and the Motor City was running on high octane. The man who had delivered the timely base hit—Leon Allen "Goose" Goslin—stood on the infield dirt and watched the stadium erupt. His big, open, farmboy face warmed to the moment. Nearly fifteen years earlier, he had exchanged the countryside around Salem, New Jersey, for the manicured turf of big league ballparks. Now it was October 7, 1935, and though America was mired in the Depression, the Goose was golden.

By the time Goose Goslin died in 1971, the Industrial Revolution had energized and then abandoned towns like Salem. But when Leon Goslin arrived with the twentieth century, smokestacks were just beginning to join silos in southwestern New Jersey. Goslin Sr. was a sharecropper, subject to the whims of the harvest, and the future Goose of the American League (a gosling is a young goose, and sports scribes of the day rarely resisted alliteration) left school after the fourth grade to assist his father in the fields. Later, Goose worked as a glassblower in Salem, and when the United States entered World War I, he manned the assembly line at the DuPont gunpowder plant in Carneys Point across the Delaware River from Wilmington. A local baseball league helped fill his idle hours, and the sturdy teenager caught the eye of professional umpire Bill McGowan, who encouraged him to go south to the minor leagues.

"Mom worked as a tomato peeler at the Heinz factory in town, and she loaned him the money to go," younger brother Jim recalled. "He went down as a pitcher, but they found out he could hit, and made an outfielder out of him. . . . He was a natural."

Yeah, Goose Goslin could hit. Playing for a team in Columbia, South Carolina, in 1921, he led the "Sally League" in runs scored, runs batted in, hits, and batting average. Scouting in the hinterlands, Washington Senators owner Clark Griffith liked the cut of the aggressive Goslin and brought him on board for the then princely sum of six thousand dollars. Later doormats in the American League, the Senators were an imposing bunch in the 1920s. They defeated John McGraw and his New York Giants in the 1924 World Series—the final fall classic for the legendary manager—and won a return trip the following year. In the

*Goose Goslin was one of baseball's finest
hitters in an era that featured the titans of the game.*
PHOTOGRAPH COURTESY OF
THE SOUTHERN NEW JERSEY ALL SPORTS MUSEUM AND HALL OF FAME

seventh game at Pittsburgh's Forbes Field, overpowering Washington pitcher Walter "The Big Train" Johnson was hampered by a leg injury, and the game ended with Goose Goslin striking out.

But Goslin—a line-drive hitter rather than an authentic slugger—had crashed three home runs in each of the 1924 and 1925 series, and become one of the premier hitters in the big leagues. His crouching, challenging stance invited the brushback (his brother called him "fearless" at the plate), but enabled him to attack any pitch close to the strike zone. And his 185 pounds, solidly distributed over a five-foot-eleven-inch frame, generated extra-base power.

When the Senators competed in the World Series, the Goslin family clambered aboard eldest brother Russell's automobile and motored south to the capital. Jim Goslin remembered bunking in a suite at Washington's Wardman Park Hotel, where chauffeurs pulled up aside dancing fountains. By day, he sat in the dugout at Griffith Stadium. It was heady stuff for a kid from Salem.

Players of that era were less handsomely remunerated than the walking mints that patrol today's domed carpets, but after a few years, Goose was doing well enough to drive his Pierce Arrow all the way to Florida for spring training. During the off-season, he lived with his sister in Salem and hunted pheasants, rabbits, and quail. Soon, he bought a two-hundred-acre farm, complete with duck meadow, three miles away in Lower Penns Neck. He eventually sold that farm and bought a small marina in Bayside, a few miles south of the site of today's Salem nuclear generating station. There, Goose lived in a makeshift building and docked forty-four rowboats for crabbers to ferry into the mouth of Stowe Creek. He added a bait shop and an icehouse and ran his business in the black.

Some years later, Atlantic City Electric was gobbling up farms and marshland on Delaware Bay, and Goslin parted with his twenty acres for a tidy fifty thousand dollars. By this time, he had retired from baseball, married, and moved to Glassboro.

The Senators returned to the World Series in 1933 (the Giants prevailed this time in five games), and Goslin homered once more. He was thirty-three now, however, and the big years seemed to be over. The fiery

Cochrane, once the team leader on Connie Mack's Philadelphia Athletics, wanted an extra veteran bat in his Detroit lineup, and the Goose became a Tiger in 1934, promptly rewarding his manager's confidence by helping the club to a pennant. Cochrane's judgment seemed even keener a year later on that October afternoon when Goslin smacked the clincher that made the Tigers world champions, lighting up the city and turning himself—however briefly—into a celebrity.

Following the 1935 series, Goslin hit the equivalent of the talk-show circuit in that pre-Letterman age, appearing onstage at the Fox theaters in Detroit and New York to field questions from fans. For this star turn, he was paid ten thousand dollars—as much as his Tiger salary. But the Goose was approaching that inevitable stage when the bat loses its thunder. He played two more seasons in Detroit and finished his big league career back in Washington as a part-time player in 1938, then spent the next two years as player-manager of a minor league franchise in Trenton. Before the advent of endorsements and television "color" commentary, ball players simply stayed ball players—or returned to work the farm, the store, the mines.

This much is certain: from 1922 through 1936, Goose Goslin was one of the most productive players in baseball. He won an AL batting championship and led the league in triples twice and RBIs once. He drove in more than a hundred runs in eleven seasons, leading his team nine times in that department. He also hit over .300 in eleven seasons (over .290 in three others); he paced his club in batting average six times and in home runs eleven times. In all, he had 8,654 official at-bats plus 948 walks in 2,287 games; drove in 1,609 runs; slugged 248 homers; and hit safely 2,735 times for a lifetime average of .316. That's staying power.

Cooperstown belatedly summoned him in 1968, three decades after his playing career had ended. Goose Goslin, by then a widower, drifted from baseball and business to the tiny South Jersey community of Roadstown near Bridgeton. His final years may have been tougher than facing Babe Ruth and Lou Gehrig at Yankee Stadium.

"He was a likable, friendly chap," his brother remembered. "But the hard life of baseball hardened him. He got on the road to drinking and couldn't leave it alone. He smoked a lot, and got throat cancer . . . had an operation and lost his voice. That took all the starch out of him, and he didn't last too long."

Goose Goslin lasted until May 1971 and is largely forgotten today.

Fans live in the moment, and athletic exploits quickly fade into yesterday's newsprint. When the game they played was a simpler, if far more autocratic enterprise, players like Goose roamed the baseball landscape. They left their plows and factories for ballparks of dirt, and grass, and steel girders that propped the roof and blocked the view. They lived in boarding houses, played in the daylight, traveled by train, bulged their cheeks with tobacco, and signed autographs on scraps of paper . . . for free. They bore wacky or florid nicknames and captured a nation's fancy.

They had their moments.

Spring Training at the Shore

Charley McManus and Walter Owens walked across the baseball diamond at Bader Field in Atlantic City, anticipating the difficult task ahead of them. It was February of 1944 and a cold wind blew in from the Atlantic Ocean as they surveyed the condition of the pock-marked infield and rock-hard outfield.

Across the ocean, the Allied forces prepared for the Normandy invasion of Nazi-occupied Europe. For McManus, superintendent of New York's Yankee Stadium, and Owens, the stadium groundskeeper, their job seemed only slightly less daunting. They had to prepare Bader Field for the arrival of the world champion New York Yankees, who would begin spring training in less than a month, in a time and place better suited for ice hockey than the national pastime.

Like most facets of American life, baseball was not immune to the changes brought about by World War II after Japan attacked Pearl Harbor. In a January 1942 letter to President Franklin D. Roosevelt, baseball commissioner Kenesaw Mountain Landis had offered to cancel baseball for the duration of the war if it would serve the national interest. Roosevelt turned him down.

"I honestly feel that it would be best for the country to keep baseball going," stated Roosevelt. "There will be fewer people unemployed and everybody will work longer hours and harder than ever before. And that means they ought to have a chance for recreation and taking their minds off their work even more than before."

While the games continued, Landis saw to it that baseball would do its part for the war effort. After the 1942 season, he ordered spring training to be held at sites north of the Potomac River and no further west than the Mississippi River to curtail unnecessary travel and conserve gasoline. The sixteen Major League clubs, which had trained in Florida, California, and Cuba in 1942, scrambled to find new facilities.

The Yankees, who had trained in Fort Lauderdale, Florida, for eighteen straight springs, set up training camp in Asbury Park in 1943. The team moved to Atlantic City for spring training in 1944 and 1945 because of the resort's facilities and hopes for slightly warmer weather.

New Jersey would prove to be popular with the Major Leagues. The Boston Red Sox held spring training at Ansley Park in Pleasantville and stayed at the Claridge Hotel in Atlantic City. In Ocean County, the New York Giants trained in Lakewood and the players and coaches got an unexpected bonus. They stayed in John D. Rockefeller's forty-six-room mansion equipped with seventeen bedrooms. In Atlantic City, the Yankees had to settle for rooms at the Senator Hotel. The three teams, along with the Philadelphia Phillies, who trained in Wilmington, Delaware, played against each other in the exhibition season.

At Bader Field, bleachers were erected for the fans and a heated and glass-enclosed press box was built to accommodate up to fifty sportswriters. By early March 1944, fourteen workers were added to the labor crew to speed up work at the field and smooth an outfield rendered bumpy by snow and subfreezing temperatures. Wary of the weather, Yankee management also secured use of the 112th Field Artillery Armory to be utilized for indoor workouts during inclement weather. Six inches of soil were put down to allow ball players to throw, bunt, and jog on a simulated baseball field.

Yankee Manager Joe McCarthy was philosophical about it all. "We will have to make the best of things along with the rest of the clubs."

While a substitute field and facilities could be found, there was no way to replace the baseball stars who had been drafted or volunteered for military service in Europe and the South Pacific. More than three hundred Major Leaguers interrupted their careers to join the armed forces. The Red Sox lost Ted Williams, the last player to hit over .400, plus all-star second-baseman Bobby Doerr. The Yankees were without future Hall-of-Famers Joe DiMaggio, Bill Dickey, and Phil Rizzuto. A player's draft status—be it 1A or 4F—was talked about as much as a

*Joe DiMaggio of the New York Yankees missed spring training in
Atlantic City in 1944 and 1945 because he was in the army. He
celebrated his return to baseball in April 1946 by hitting a home run at
Shibe Park in Philadelphia against the Philadelphia Athletics.*

PHOTOGRAPH COURTESY OF THE *COURIER-POST*

hitter's batting average or a pitcher's earned-run average. Baseball rosters were the equivalent of a cast of understudies in a play.

"We have a field," observed chief Yankee scout Paul Krichell on the eve of spring training in 1944. "Now all we need are enough players to fill it."

Spring training got off to a soggy debut when a March 13 storm dumped 1.86 inches of rain, turning the outdoor field into a quagmire and forcing the Yankees to train indoors at the armory for six straight days before returning to Bader Field on March 26 with exhibition season starting on April 1.

Despite the weather, McCarthy was pleased with what he saw. "I know seashore weather is unpredictable, but we're on the ball field two to three hours a day. It's a swell hotel, probably the best we've been in during a training season, and everyone is treating us fine. They're the things that count."

While southern New Jersey was not southern Florida, spring training in Atlantic City was a success for both the Yankees and the local population. Baseball served as a morale booster for civilians and the military stationed in the region.

Some residents got to play bit parts with the Yankees. Pleasantville Councilman Claude Larned was pressed into service as an emergency catcher. A former minor league player, he had written to the Yankees to volunteer his services, and the team had accepted. Raymond Trumpi, thirteen, of Atlantic City, was the envy of classmates after being chosen as the Yankee batboy.

During their stay, the Yankees assisted in the war effort, visiting servicemen at England General Hospital and other military hospitals in the region. The Red Cross accepted donations of cigarettes, chocolate, and food from civilians who attended the team's workouts.

The exhibition games gave fans a preview of the coming season. The Yankees and Phillies played the first-ever Major League game in Atlantic City on April 1, 1944. Some 2,678 fans, including 300 servicemen, turned out to see the Yankees top the Phillies, 5–4, behind a home run by Yankee outfielder Johnny Lindell. Perhaps inspired by the chilly weather, the teams took just one hour and fifty-two minutes to play the contest.

The next day, four thousand people watched the Yankees edge the Brooklyn Dodgers, 4–3 in eleven innings, in a rematch of the 1941 World

Series. Bader Field proved to be a good-luck charm for the Yankees as they posted a 6–1 won-loss record in 1944.

McCarthy announced on April 10 that the Yankees would return to Atlantic City in 1945 if the northern training rule remained in effect. Not only did they return, they were accompanied by the Red Sox, their longtime American League rival.

The war continued to thin out the talent on Major League rosters. By 1945, the Yankees had twenty-nine players in their organization in military service while the Red Sox had twenty-eight. Teams scrambled to sign any available talent. The Red Sox signed Jim McDonald, a seventeen-year-old, to bolster their roster. The Cincinnati Reds had used Joe Nuxhall, a fifteen-year-old pitcher, in 1944, while the St. Louis Browns used Pete Gray, a one-armed outfielder, for seventy-seven games in 1945.

The Yankees switched their indoor practice facility to a hangar at Bader Field in 1945. The winter proved to be milder than the previous year's. At one point in March, the Red Sox held outdoor workouts for nine straight days. "We've had twice as much batting practice as we did for two weeks last spring [in Massachusetts]," said Red Sox manager Joe Cronin.

Travel restrictions imposed by Commissioner Landis resulted in the Yankees and Red Sox playing each other in nine exhibition games— six at Bader Field and three at Ansley Park in Pleasantville.

It helped set up a heated rivalry that would continue in the years after World War II. Their first game on March 31 saw a strong wind blowing at Bader Field, as the Yankees edged the Red Sox, 15–14, with a five-run rally in the ninth. In the first exhibition game at Pleasantville on April 3, the Red Sox gained a measure of revenge by topping the Yankees, 6–4, before a thousand fans. The series was hard fought, and the Yankees won five of the nine games. By the time the final game was played at Bader Field on April 8, there were signs that spring training would return to Florida and other warmer climates in 1946.

Professional baseball in Atlantic City would fade into memory but would be revived half a century later with the Atlantic City Surf playing minor league baseball in the Sandcastle. Nevertheless, South Jersey's contributions to the game would be part of an unlikely chapter in the history of Major League baseball.

Clamshell Pitching: One Singular Sand-sation

D espite its size, New Jersey has racked up an impressive lineup of athletic achievements. The Garden State was the site of the first professional baseball game played with nine players on a side and a published box score—the Knickerbockers and the New York Nine in Hoboken in 1846; the first collegiate football game—Princeton vs. Rutgers in New Brunswick in 1869; and the first champion in the first professional basketball league—Trenton Nationals of the National League of Professional Basketball in 1899.

New Jersey is also the home of halls of fame in sports ranging from golf in Far Hills, to bicycling in Somerville, to marbles in Wildwood.

One sport with strong ties to South Jersey has flowered under the athletic radar screen for more than half a century. Clamshell pitching is an unlikely candidate for coverage in *Sports Illustrated* or ESPN's "SportsCenter," but, in Cape May, it is as much a part of the city's heritage as Victorian architecture or bed-and-breakfast inns.

Since 1946, the International Clamshell Pitching Club of Cape May has sponsored an annual tournament on the beach in either late August or early September, depending on the tidal conditions of the Atlantic Ocean. The tournaments have drawn more than a hundred competitors in the junior, men's, and women's divisions during some years.

"The beauty of clamshell pitching is that, unlike tennis, bowling, or ice hockey, it's an easy game to play," said Rich Reinhart, club president and former champion who began competing in 1971. "Unlike horseshoes, the best players are not going to shoot 95 percent ringers and blow everybody else away."

Clamshell pitching has elements of horseshoes and quoits. Two holes are dug in the hard-packed sand on the beach. The holes are twenty-five feet, six inches apart and five inches in diameter. Each players throws two shells toward one of the holes. A shell in the hole counts as two points, but if both players' shells are in the hole, they cancel each other out. Score one point for the closer of the two remaining shells to the hole. A game is played to twenty-one points and a player must win by two points.

"The first clamshell pitchers were probably American Indians before the arrival of the white man," Reinhart said. Clamshell pitching was done informally on the beaches in Cape May in the 1920s and 1930s and the years during World War II.

Jim Stevens, a Cape May resident, credited Dr. Jonathan Miller, a Philadelphia dentist, with organizing the first tournament in 1946. Stevens, who served in the navy during the war, quickly became proficient at the sport and entered the first tournament.

"We had about thirty people and played singles and doubles," Stevens recalled. He was the first singles champion at the age of twenty-two and became a fixture at the event, having participated in every tournament since.

Now seventy-seven, Stevens credited the quality of the hard-packed sand on the Cape May beaches and the easy availability of shells with contributing to the rise of the sport. "Some years, you could go to the ocean's edge and find your shells on the day of the tournament."

Shells, of course, played a key role in a player's success in the tournament. Breaking shells during the play was always a possibility. According to the rules of the tournament, a broken shell remains in play as long as two-thirds of it is intact. "We had many an argument over that rule," Stevens said, chuckling over the memory. "You could break half a dozen shells in the course of a match."

In the latter years of the tournament, shell availability began to decline. To conserve their supply, some players used artificial shells made in molds. "Artificial shells use a hard plastic with metal filings added for weight," Reinhart said.

The size of the shells was an important factor as well. "The shells should be about four inches long, two inches wide, and weigh about four ounces," Reinhart said. Some players decorate their shells. Reinhardt painted his red, white, and blue with stars. "I started it for the bicentennial year [of 1976]," he said.

A sense of fun and a sense of humor have been essential elements in the tournament's longevity.

Stevens recalled Steve Steger, a longtime coach at a local high school, who would lead the tournament competitors in calisthenics and deep-knee bends. "Then he would lead them in finger exercises," Stevens said. "We'd draw a good crowd of people on the beach wondering, What are these goof-offs doing?"

Occasionally, the tournament took on a European flavor when a visitor from Great Britain or Germany would compete. "We had an Englishman named Duke Fairburn compete and served tea during the break," Stevens said. When a German competed, beer was served during the break to make the visitor feel at home in Cape May.

"That's why we were international," Stevens said, referring to the club's name. Other international competitors included residents of Canada and Australia.

During some years, an off-season banquet was held at the Penn Sheraton Hotel in Philadelphia. To keep their skills in shape, club members would pack beach sand in their car trunks and take it to the roof of the hotel where a makeshift pitching area would be set up. Before the banquet, a few games of clamshell pitching would be held with a view of Philadelphia, instead of the Atlantic Ocean.

Over the years, participants in the tournament ranged from weekend warriors to professional athletes. Representing the latter was Bosh Pritchard, a running back for the Philadelphia Eagles, who played in three NFL championship games and helped the Eagles win NFL titles in 1948 and 1949. The son-in-law of Dr. Miller, Pritchard found that talent on the gridiron did not translate into victory on the beach, as he never won a singles championship.

In its fifty-four years, tournament organizers have changed with the times. Women began competing in the 1960s. A separate category was later added for children and teenagers. The tournament grew to three days with young people competing on the first day and men and women competing in singles, doubles, and mixed doubles over the final two days. The idea behind the tournament for children was to create interest in the sport among the young generation, and the concept proved to be successful.

"We've had at least three people win both the junior and senior tournaments," Reinhart said.

During the 1990s tournament organizers decided to pay tribute to the best players by starting a Clamshell Pitching Hall of Fame. So far, ten men and five women have been inducted.

With the arrival of a new century, the future of the tournament is at a crossroads. Erosion of the beach in Cape May has led to beach replenishment programs. However, the effort to save the beach now jeopardizes the tournament's future.

"The offshore sand pumped in is very granular and cannot mold into a proper hard-sand hole for the game," Reinhart explained. "The high waterfront dunes [that were] created have contained the fifty-yard high tides that formerly left a broad expanse of hard-packed Cape May sand," he added.

As a result, interest in the tournament declined and the adult competition was canceled in 2000; the one-day youth tournament was held.

Reinhart said the club will consider its options in trying to keep the tournament alive in the twenty-first century, such as moving the tournament to a new site in Cape May. Club members are hoping the sands of time have not run out on one of Cape May's summertime sporting traditions.

Bridgeton at Bat

Dickie Noles toes the pitching mound as he peers at his catcher for the signal. The former member of the Philadelphia Phillies is wearing the orange and white of Gildea's Raiders, not the more familiar red-and-white striped Phillies uniform he donned when he helped the team win its only World Series in 1980.

Fifteen years later, the competitive juices flow just as freely as he pitches for the Wilmington team in the first-round game at the twenty-ninth annual Bridgeton Invitational Baseball Tournament. Staked to a 6–0 lead, Noles struggles in the fourth inning as he gives up two runs to the Myles Transportation team from Cinnaminson, Burlington County. Two runners are on base with two outs as Noles faces the next hitter. Working the count to 2–2, Noles appears to strike out the hitter on a fastball that nicks the outside corner. The umpire disagrees, calling it a ball.

"Hey, ump, wake up," a fan shouts from the stands at Alden Field, his voice rising in derision as others around him second the command.

Noles shows no displeasure with the umpire's call. Summoning a little more energy, he rears back and strikes the batter out on a 3–2 fastball. Noles walks off the mound to the cheers of the crowd, one more memorable moment in the history of the Bridgeton tournament.

Now in its thirty-fifth year, the two-week tournament brings a taste of minor league baseball to South Jersey, featuring teams from New

Gerry Alden (left), Phillies Hall of Famer Richie Ashburn (second from right), and Ben Lynch (right) present a plaque to umpire Bernice Gera at the Bridgeton Invitational Tournament. After Gera died, part of her ashes were scattered on Alden Field, because she enjoyed her time spent at the tournament.

PHOTOGRAPH COURTESY OF
THE SOUTHERN NEW JERSEY ALL SPORTS MUSEUM AND HALL OF FAME

York State to Washington, D.C. In an era where the national pastime is marked by player strikes and inflated egos and salaries, the tournament is a refreshing reminder of what the sport used to be.

The Bridgeton Invitational pitches to its fans tradition, in its natural grass field; intimacy, in the twenty-five-hundred-seat Alden Field; and economy, since a family of four can park the car and attend a nightly doubleheader for under ten dollars. With hot dogs selling for a dollar and sodas at seventy-five cents, a trip to the refreshment stand doesn't require taking out a loan.

A *Bull Durham* atmosphere prevails at the tournament with the emphasis on family entertainment. Trivia contests are held between games, with questions focusing on tournament history and South Jersey athletes. Door prizes are given away with each home run. "Another Ed's Body Shop Blast," the public address announcer proclaims, referring to a local business that has offered up more than one giveaway in the name of good old-fashioned American sales. Hear the name enough and next time your car needs repairs, where will you think to go?

With all the sidelights, the tournament's selling point remains the game itself.

"The level of play is Class A minor league," said Bob Rose, former tournament chair and director of Bridgeton's recreation and public affairs department. "On a good night, it can be class AA."

"This is people playing for the love of the game," declares Ben Lynch, a member of the tournament's board of directors.

That love of the game has served the tournament well—on and off the field—since its inception in 1967. Overall attendance for the history of the tournament has exceeded one million people, a testament to the hard-working volunteers who turn out each summer.

The idea for the annual tournament was born after Bridgeton hosted the 1962 Babe Ruth World Series, a national baseball tournament for teenage teams. It was then that Bridgeton officials thought of the invitational, to be played each August, as a way to help fill a gap in the city's social calendar between the Fourth of July and Labor Day. The first tournament featured six South Jersey teams playing in a double-elimination tournament, in which a team is eliminated from competition after losing twice.

Except for the cast of players and the number of teams participating, the tournament has remained largely unchanged over the years. The tournament now features sixteen teams—eight from South Jersey and the remainder from outside the region. The winners in each division play for the title in a best two-out-of-three series.

"I don't think the organizers thought the tournament would take off the way it did," said Rose, forty-seven, who sold sodas at the original tournament and worked up his way up through the ranks to become tournament chair. "Nobody thought the tournament would last twenty-five years."

Asked about the growth of minor league teams, in Trenton, Wilmington, and Atlantic City, Rose is unfazed, insisting the recent infusion of baseball in the region has not hurt the tournament. The Trenton Thunder and Wilmington Blue Rocks have supported the event over the years, even donating souvenirs for door prizes.

The success of the Bridgeton Invitational led the New York Mets to consider placing a minor league franchise in the Cumberland County city in the early 1970s, Rose said. The idea was dropped because the team wanted exclusive use of Alden Field, Bridgeton's main ball field.

Rose and his staff have learned to deal with the unexpected. In 1995, a meteorological curveball was thrown at the tournament when a tornado hit Alden Field early on the morning of July 16. Four lighting standards were broken; the press box, sound system, and part of the bleachers also were damaged. Like a team trailing in the ninth inning, the community rallied to repair the field. The city council made an emergency appropriation to replace the lights. The start of the tournament was delayed four days, but when the lights came on for the first time, there was an audible sigh followed by a round of cheers from the stands. Rose, who resembled a Broadway director watching his production on opening night, allowed himself a smile. "This is the first time we had problems before a tournament started."

While the players change from year to year, Alden Field has remained the centerpiece of the tournament. The field resembles an outdoor cathedral with the stands serving as the pews for the baseball faithful. The field has close-cut green grass and trees just beyond the outfield fence, making it a perfect backdrop for hitters. Fans are close to the field and have to be alert for foul balls whizzing into the stands.

The front row of seats behind the first and third base dugouts are close enough for fans to see beads of sweat glistening on a ball player's neck. Spectators listening can eavesdrop on conversations between ball players. "C'mon, hit the cutoff man!" a shortstop barked to one of his outfielders after the player returned to the dugout after the end of an inning. Players can be heard discussing an opposing pitcher ("Watch for his slider!") or offering encouragement as a teammate goes up to bat ("You can hit this guy!").

The field earns high praise from the players. "This is a beautiful field," said Jeff Robinson, twenty, a catcher for Pleasantville, as he waited to play in the final game of a Friday night triple-header in August 1995.

"It's an honor to play in front of this many people," the Cape May resident said, gesturing to the stands as they continued to fill. Robinson, who played for the Rowan College team in Glassboro, admitted he was unaccustomed to playing in front of a large crowd. "If you would have twenty people for a regular game [at Rowan], that would be a good night."

Tournament organizers have respected baseball tradition without

A pitcher, catcher, and batter wait for the umpire's call at the Bridgeton Invitational Baseball Tournament.
PHOTOGRAPH COURTESY OF THE SOUTHERN NEW JERSEY ALL SPORTS MUSEUM AND
HALL OF FAME

forgoing innovation. Bernice Gera, who tried unsuccessfully to become the first woman to umpire in the Major Leagues, accepted an invitation to umpire in the tournament in the early 1970s. After fighting the Major League establishment, Gera enjoyed the encouragement she found in Bridgeton and continued to umpire there for several years. Gera paid Bridgeton and the tournament the ultimate compliment. After her death at the age of sixty-one in 1992, part of her ashes were scattered along the third-base line at Alden Field.

The tournament has been in the forefront of other innovations as well. In 1969, the tournament adopted the designated hitter rule, four years before the American League did so. Speed-up rules have been adopted, too; a pitcher must start his windup twenty seconds after receiving the ball or a ball is called. Pitchers are also limited to three warmup tosses per inning.

"We feel the speed-up rules help the fans stay involved, since the games are shorter, and we always have two games a night," Lynch said.

Another feature of the tournament now brings former Major Leaguers to town. Former big leaguers who have played in the tournament after their careers ended include Noles; Jim Bouton of the New York Yankees; and Tug McGraw, Randy Lerch, and Al Holland, all pitchers on pennant-winning teams for the Phillies in the early 1980s. Bridgeton has had its fair share of young players who went on to play in the majors, including Andre Thornton, Jeff Manto, and John Montefusco.

"I like being on the mound with a ball in my hand," said Bouton, who pitched on a semiprofessional level into his fifties. His baseball diary, *Ball Four*, has sold more than five million copies.

Rose credits Bouton's appearance with the Trenton Pat Pavers in 1970 with giving the tournament national visibility.

Noles echoes Bouton's sentiments about pitching. "I still love the game," says Noles, who still maintains the slim physique of a ball player at age forty-four. "You don't see a lot of [former ball players] play. Many of them have had enough or let their pride get in the way."

Noles intends to return to pitch in the tournament again. Why? It's as simple as a fastball down the middle. "I like the people associated with this organization," he said. His enjoyment is evident after a game as he walks along the stands, stopping to talk to fans or sign an autograph for a youngster.

The tournament continues to inspire loyalty. Take William Sumiel, seventy, of Salem, who, at the age of forty-two, pitched for Salem County, the first team to win the tournament in 1967. Sumiel pitched for seven years and has since made the transition from player to spectator.

"You got to have pitching to win this tournament," he observed in 1995 after watching a pitcher give up three walks followed by a grand slam. In the stands, Sumiel used a cane to get around, tapping it on the ground in time with an internal rhythm and occasionally using it as a chin rest.

The tournament can get in your blood and stay there. Like the swallows returning every spring to San Juan Capistrano, the boys of summer will return to Bridgeton in August, and baseball fans will rise up and cheer.

Bibliography

Anderson, Norman D. *Ferris Wheels, an Illustrated History*. Bowling Green, Ohio: The Popular Press, 1992.

Armstrong, Harry, and Tom Wilk. *New Jersey Firsts*. Philadelphia: Camino Books, 1999.

Bergreen, Laurence. *Capone: The Man and the Era*. New York: Simon & Schuster, 1994.

Butler, Frank. *Book of the Boardwalk*. Atlantic City, N.J.: Atlantic City Board of Education, 1952.

Cain Tim. *Peck's Beach*. Harvey Cedars, N.J.: Down the Shore Publishing, 1988.

DiClerico, James M., and Barry J. Pavelec. *The Jersey Game: The History of Modern Baseball from Its Birth to the Big Leagues in the Garden State*. New Brunswick, N.J.: Rutgers University Press, 1991.

Dudley, William S. *The Naval War of 1812*, vol. 2. Washington, D.C.: Naval Historical Center, 1992.

English, A. L. *History of Atlantic City, New Jersey*. Atlantic City, N.J.: Dickson and Gilling, 1884.

Francis, David, and Diane Francis. *Wildwood by the Sea*. Fairview, Ohio: Amusement Park Books, 1998.

French, Samuel Gibbs. *Two Wars: The Autobiography and Diary of Gen. Samuel G. French, CSA*. 1901. Reprint ed. Huntington, W.Va.: Blue Acorn Press, 1999.

Funnell, Charles E. *By the Beautiful Sea*. New York: Knopf, 1975.

Haley, John W., and John von Hoelle. *Sound and Glory*. Wilmington, Del.: Dyne-American Publishing, 1990.

Holway, John. *Blackball Stars: Negro League Pioneers*. Westport, Conn.: Meckler, 1988.

Jonathan Pitney, M.D.—Fifty Years of Progress on the Coast of New Jersey. 1886.

Kelly, William E. *Birth of the Birdie*. West Berlin, N.J.: Innovative Publishing, 1997.

Levi, Vicki Gold, and Lee Eisenberg. *Atlantic City, 125 Years of Ocean Madness*. Berkeley, Calif.: Ten Speed Press, 1994.

Levy, Shawn. *King of Comedy*. New York: St. Martin's, 1996.

McMahon, William. *History Gardner's Basin, Atlantic City*. Atlantic City, N.J.: Atlantic County Historical Waterfront and William McMahon, 1976.

———. *South Jersey Towns—History and Legend*. New Brunswick, N.J.: Rutgers University Press, 1973.

———. *So Young, So Gay*. Atlantic City, N.J.: Atlantic City Press, 1970.

Santelli, Robert. *Aquarius Rising: The Rock Festival Years*. New York: Delta, 1980.

Schoenberg, Robert J. *Mr. Capone*. New York: Morrow, 1992.

Tosches, Nick. *Dino: Living High in the Dirty Business of Dreams*. Garden City, N.Y.: Doubleday, 1992.

Index

About the Authors

Jim Waltzer has written for *Atlantic City* magazine, *New Jersey Monthly*, and various other regional and national magazines. He is a published fiction writer and newspaper editor.

Tom Wilk is a copy editor at the *Courier-Post* in Cherry Hill, New Jersey. He is the co-author, with Harry Armstrong, of *New Jersey Firsts: The Famous, Infamous and Quirky of the Garden State*. He has written for *Atlantic City* magazine, *New Jersey Monthly*, and *No Depression* magazine. He lives in Pitman, New Jersey.